CULTURE AND THE RESTRUCTURING OF COMMUNITY MENTAL HEALTH

Recent Titles in
Contributions in Psychology

Ecological Beliefs and Behaviors: Assessment and Change
David B. Gray in collaboration with Richard J. Borden and Russell H. Weigel

Sexuality: New Perspectives
Zira DeFries, Richard C. Friedman, and Ruth Corn, editors

Portrait and Story: Dramaturgical Approaches to the Study of Persons
Larry Cochran

The Meaning of Grief: A Dramaturgical Approach to Understanding Emotion
Larry Cochran and Emily Claspell

New Ideas in Therapy: Introduction to an Interdisciplinary Approach
Douglas H. Ruben and Dennis J. Delprato, editors

Human Consciousness and Its Evolution: A Multidimensional View
Richard W. Coan

From AI to Zeitgeist: A Philosophical Guide for the Skeptical Psychologist
N. H. Pronko

Inevitability: Determinism, Fatalism, and Destiny
Leonard W. Doob

The Psychology of Writing: The Affective Experience
Alice Glarden Brand

Medieval Psychology
Simon Kemp

Hesitation: Impulsivity and Reflection
Leonard W. Doob

CULTURE AND THE RESTRUCTURING OF COMMUNITY MENTAL HEALTH

William A. Vega
&
John W. Murphy

CONTRIBUTIONS IN PSYCHOLOGY, NUMBER 16

GREENWOOD PRESS
NEW YORK • WESTPORT, CONNECTICUT • LONDON

Library of Congress Cataloging-in-Publication Data

Vega, William.
Culture and the restructuring of community mental health / William A. Vega and John W. Murphy.
p. cm.—(Contributions in psychology, ISSN 0736–2714 ; no. 16)
Includes bibliographical references.
ISBN 0–313–26887–8 (lib. bdg. : alk. paper)
1. Community mental health services—United States. 2. Mental health policy–United States. 3. Minorities—Mental health services—United States. 4. Urban poor—Mental health services—United States. I. Murphy, John W. II. Title. III. Series.
[DNLM: 1. Community Mental Health Services—organization & administration. 2. Cultural Deprivation. 3. Minority Groups.
W1 CO778NHH no. 16 / WA 305 V422c]
RA790.6.V44 1990
362.2′2′0973—dc20
DLC 90–3158

British Library Cataloguing in Publication Data is available.

Library of Congress Catalog Card Number: 90–3158
ISBN: 0–313–26887–8
ISSN: 0736–2714

First published in 1990

Greenwood Press, 88 Post Road West, Westport, CT 06881
An imprint of Greenwood Publishing Group, Inc.

Printed in the United States of America

The paper used in this book complies with the Permanent Paper Standard issued by the National Information Standards Organization (Z39.48–1984).

10 9 8 7 6 5 4 3 2 1

Contents

Chapter One:
Critical Junctures in the Community Mental Health Movement 1

Chapter Two:
Theory Development in the Early Days 21

Chapter Three:
The Philosophical and Conceptual Basis of Community-Based Analysis 43

Chapter Four:
Medicalization and the Degradation of Culture 61

Chapter Five:
Reconceptualizing Knowledge, Order, Illness, and Intervention 85

Chapter Six:
Proyecto Bienestar: An Example of a Community-Based Intervention 103

Chapter Seven:
Programmatic Changes and Citizen Involvement 123

Chapter Eight:
The Political Side of Community-Based Policies 141

Selected Annotated Bibliography 155

Index 159

CULTURE AND THE RESTRUCTURING OF COMMUNITY MENTAL HEALTH

Chapter One

Critical Junctures in the Community Mental Health Movement

Introduction

This book is about mental health care, especially for cultural minorities and the urban poor. This segment of the U.S. population is rapidly increasing in size and heterogeneity. The challenge for services providers is to find new access methods and to develop appropriate and effective interventions. Yet at present there is little evidence that this new frontier for public mental health will receive systematic attention. A unique era is ending, and the intellectual and financial resources that have driven reform in community mental health for the previous three decades appear to be exhausted. Federal leadership has ebbed, biomedical and psychopharmacological research has become *de rigueur*, to the detriment of social and community psychiatry, and the training of mental health professionals continues in a decidedly "traditional" mode.

A remarkable transformation has been witnessed in public mental health services over the past thirty years. Several convergent trends have prompted these changes, and these trends will be discussed in this chapter. Nonetheless, one fact has remained consistent over this time period: cultural minorities in the United States have failed to receive adequate mental health care. Although the specifics vary by group, survey data indicate that the needs of minorities are largely unmet,[1] and, when services are available, too often inappropriate care is received.[2] Also evident is that current patterns in research and professional preparation serve to perpetuate these tendencies.[3] The purpose of this book is to examine the important lessons that should have been experienced during the previous three decades of experimentation, and to lay the theoretical foundation for a future public mental health system that is more responsive to the needs of cultural minorities. This is not to say the field is moribund. Fortunately, several committed researchers and practitioners continue to create new knowledge, interventions, and treatments, despite very scarce resources.

If the past is prologue for the future, important benefits should be gained from the study of history. However, the unfolding of the community mental health movement, as well as its relationship to cultural minorities and their mental health needs, is not well understood. Certainly, from its inception the community mental health movement intended to serve the needs of cultural minorities, but the implications of offering services to such a complex population were not initially appreciated. Only when the community mental health movement reached its midpoint did minority mental health arise as a subspecialty, or "mini-movement," among researchers and practitioners. Albeit unintended, this may turn out to be one of the most enduring intellectual legacies of the era.

Four dominant factors have affected the ability of mental health professionals to address the needs of cultural minorities. These are: (1) fluctuations in the political climate and financial support for services; (2) confusion about goals and methods in community mental health; (3) the limited knowledge base about community and cultural characteristics used for training practitioners and designing interventions; and (4) broad changes in the composition, diversity, and size of cultural minority groups. Taken together, these factors have undermined the prospects of equitable and effective mental health services for all citizens. The irony of this situation, as pointed out by Arthur Kleinman, is that the mental health establishment has returned to a very narrow disease model of mental illness at the very moment that social models of health are most needed.[4] Paradoxically, social models of intervention are finally gaining some acceptance in general medicine.

The Rise of the Community Health Movement

As a point of clarification, the phrase "community mental health movement" refers specifically to broad changes in policy and institutional arrangements for the delivery of mental health services that occurred at the federal, state, and local levels between 1946 and 1981.[5] Inherent in these changes, and instrumental to their adoption, were philosophical suppositions regarding the superiority of community-based care for those who are seriously mentally ill. Additionally, the need was recognized for a broad spectrum of remedial and preventive services in order to reduce the incidence of new chronic cases among the general population. Therefore, a decidedly proactive orientation challenged the mental health establishment to engage the community. This meant moving services beyond the limited range of individual therapy, and creating new interventions designed to target the sources of personal disorganization within the social environment.

While the policy phase of the movement clearly began around 1946 with the passage of the National Mental Health Act and the funding of the National Institute of Mental Health, the deinstitutionalization phase began in the late 1950s, engendered in part by the use of more effective medications and legislation restricting involuntary detention.[6] Federally sponsored community mental health centers began to appear in the mid-1960s. The philosophical roots of community psychiatry have no absolute point of origin and can be traced back into the nineteenth century.[7] However, the most obvious precipitating influence was the large number of military recruits during World War II who were rejected for service because of alleged "neuropsychiatric problems."[8] This finding suggested that the general population of the United States had higher levels of undetected and untreated psychiatric problems than were previously assumed.

As a response to this situation, researchers began to launch large community epidemiologic studies to estimate the true prevalence of psychiatric problems. These studies succeeded in confirming earlier suspicions and, despite the use of fairly simple protocols, provided convincing evidence that a significant portion of the American population could be identified as having either a morbid or premorbid psychiatric status. The Mid-town Manhattan study, for example, found that up to 80 percent of the population studied was experiencing some psychiatric malaise, and about 20 percent was having problems considered serious enough to require treatment.[9] Although the methods used to attain these estimates have been debated, there was little disagreement with the implications. Specifically, the United States has a large subpopulation that needs psychiatric services, and people with low income are disproportionately at risk for becoming ill. Furthermore, there was no public mental health system available to address this problem other than the restricted services offered by the Veterans Administration Hospitals.

A clear progression of events led to the landmark federal Mental Health Centers Act of 1963 (Public Law 88-164). This movement was abetted by parallel activity and support in "early adopter" states such as California, where the development of community provider networks at the county level went forward in the 1950s independent of federal efforts.[10] Therefore, the community mental health movement represented a widespread effort to expand the community base of mental health services and reduce reliance on state mental hospitals. The aim was never that the government would take over the treatment of clients, even though federal agencies provided the intellectual and financial impetus for dramatically remodeling care subsequent to the Act of 1963, especially in poor states. Theoretically, the role of the federal government was to provide guidance in program innovation and evaluation, mainly through research and demonstration projects, by using the National Institute of Mental Health, and by encouraging each state to start centers by providing financial incentives.[11] For example, federal funds for constructing community mental health centers (CMHCs) and core staffing were supplied after a review of state applications, but an increasing amount of funding had to come from local sources each year following these initial grants.

The ultimate objective of the federal plan was to provide a high and uniform standard of mental health care, and a wide array of integrated services, especially in those regions which were seriously underserved. The public law that mandated the construction of CMHCs required each participating state to initiate a state plan based on a needs assessment and evaluation of existing services. Additionally, a specific state agency should be responsible for assessing how community mental health centers would affect the delivery of services to already existing patients, as well as to unserved and underserved populations. The programmatic goal was to create a network of 2000 centers nationwide, with each one serving a definable geographic service region, or "catchment area," that has a target population between 75,000 to 200,000 individuals.

The Political Context of the Community Mental Health Movement

This was obviously an ambitious undertaking, which came to fruition in the context of political idealism and social reform encouraged by the Kennedy Administration. Indeed, his report to congress in 1963 underscored the belief that the requisite knowledge, leadership, and resources were now present for a direct "assault" on mental illness. Fundamental changes should now be made in the care of the chronically mental ill, thereby moving them from the "backward" into an integrated environment of community treatment. In his address, President Kennedy also alluded to the importance of universal access to appropriate mental health care, and to the initiation of programs that would "correct the harsh environmental conditions" through a new, bold, public health-oriented configuration of services.

The political basis for community mental health legislation was facilitated by the intense social criticism, activism, and reform so characteristic of the 1960s. The Kafkaesque horrors of the mental hospital were graphically illustrated by President Kennedy in his 1963 Congressional message with the words: "hospitals and homes have been shamefully understaffed, overcrowded, unpleasant institutions from which death too often provided the only firm hope of release."[12] Books appeared, such as Ken Kesey's *One Flew over the Cuckoo's Nest*, that sensationalized the issue. A civil rights movement also was in full swing that highlighted the social contradictions in American society, and demands for reform were fueled by the moral challenges issued by both Presidents Kennedy and Johnson. At the same time, the intensifying war in Vietnam was met with equally intense opposition, which, for many, had the effect of creating a link between the need for domestic reform and the seeming wastefulness of the war abroad. It is impossible to convey in a few words the degree of disenchantment with public institutions experienced by many Americans during this period, but the net effect was to create an atmosphere that was highly charged with the spirit of reform. And the targets for social action were multiple, including the treatment of the mentally ill.

Within the more narrow professional guild, penetrating criticism had been circulating for some time about how hospital-based treatment contributed to refractory mental illness.[13] Prevailing definitions of mental illness relegated its victims to perpetual sick roles, and these labels were resistant to change.[14] In this regard, those who operated mental hospitals fulfilled their own expectations about patient behavior. Moreover, psychiatric nomenclature was often fuzzy and unreliable, and thus the social relevance of a diagnosis was clearly questionable. Worse still, psychiatric judgments were being used as a legal justification for restricting individual freedom, and thus patients' lives were permanently altered. In the social science literature, total institutions were considered best to prepare people for life in repressive surroundings.

For other writers, the essential issue was the inadequacy of traditional mental health treatment. Regardless of how available remedial services became, the mental health needs of the American population could not be met by relying on these methods. Therefore, a more public health-primary prevention model of mental health services would be needed in the future.[15] This position was intellectually appealing and morally satisfying. Implied is that the onset of some psychiatric disorders could be arrested by what Rogers called "general preventive measures directed at the determination and control of the underlying pattern of environmental relationships."[16] The empirical rationale for this kind of social intervention in mental health was derived from research such as the pioneering work of Faris and Dunham in the 1930s.[17] They found consistent relationships between social class, social disorganization, and the incidence and prevalence of treated mental disorders.[18] This knowledge combined with the rise of social stress theory in the 1950s were salient in rethinking the scope of mental health intervention as a method for lowering the risk levels of entire populations.[19]

Origins of the Social and Minority Mental Health Agenda

Part of the civil rights dialogue in the late 1960s, especially during the minority student movement on college campuses, focused on the fact that material and human resources were desperately needed to organize and improve the collective status of minority, low-income communities. The appropriate response to this situation, it was believed, included developing new human services programs and training minority professionals who could return and offer services to their communities. There was, for the first time, a significant cadre of minority students in the collegiate pipeline, because of special recruitment and financial assistance programs. Most of these students were African Americans, but increasing numbers of Hispanic and Asian students were also coming into universities. These students had several things in common. They were not traditional university students, they came from low-income backgrounds, and often they had unique social experiences and physical characteristics that distinguished them from nonminority students. A powerful "consciousness of kind" developed, which was instrumental in creating a favorable disposition toward group action and community service among minority students.

The ideological theme of this period was derived from revolutionary writers such as Frantz Fanon, Paulo Friere, and Malcolm X, who, albeit in quite dissimilar circumstances, attacked the roots of institutionalized inequality. Each writer sought to demonstrate that the process of social liberation was predicated on a proper construction of reality. This required resocialization in order to undermine the prevailing view that minorities are inferior, and to destroy the asymmetrical social relations between institutional representatives and minority group members. Oppressed people, in short, had to define their own realities. In turn, this would lead to the "empowerment" of disenfranchised persons by enabling them to participate in the social systems that directly shaped their lives. The operant term was "self-determination." This was to be achieved, in the American context, by taking control of the vital institutions affecting the health, social, and economic well-being of minority communities. Indeed, this activist ideology in many ways motivated the initial cohort of minority practitioners.[20] And this ideology was, at least in part, compatible with the social agenda of the community mental health movement.

Nonetheless, the community mental health movement never had a clear vision regarding the fusion of institutional reform with meeting the mental health needs of minorities. Since the problems of humankind were in great part social in origin, the new charge of the mental health professional was to create a more hygienic social environment.[21] Mental health professionals set about the business of transcending their traditional roles by offering a wide range of services to a much broader constituency. Furthermore, these services were to include incursions into the realm of social engineering, community organizing, and local politics. But the theoretical and operational *modus operandi* were not specified beforehand,[22] nor were the necessary planning procedures outlined with any clarity.[23] Lacking either a theoretical blue print or instructive community trials to guide their formulations, the door opened for experimentation, but also for role confusion, professional rivalries, and organizational conflicts. Mental health professionals, who had never received the training appropriate for their new obligations, were now being asked to set up shop in unfamiliar social and cultural settings, and to develop a delivery system from an array of disparate services.[24]

Attention should be paid to the fact that the Community Mental Health Centers Act of 1963 did not specifically address the issue of services for minorities, despite evidence that standard mental health services were often inappropriate for these groups, and that low-income minorities were disproportionately "at risk" for mental health problems. This legislation (Public Law 94-63) was amended practically every year after it was passed, and in 1975 the following statement was added pertaining to cultural minorities.[25] CMHCs were explicitly required to have:

1. Developed a plan and made arrangements responsive to the needs of such population for providing services to the extent practicable in the language and cultural context most appropriate to such individuals, and
2. Identified an individual on its staff who is fluent in both that language and English and whose responsibilities shall include providing guidance to such individuals and to appropriate staff members with respect to cultural sensitivities and bridging linguistic and cultural differences.

However, beyond these broad guidelines, no other requirements are mentioned pertaining to the mental health needs of minority groups. Each state was given free reign to deal individually with this issue.

Actually, the first signal from the federal government that cultural ramifications had not been adequately taken into account by the community mental health system was found in the 1978 report from the President's Commission on Mental Health.[26] This document includes detailed information about how and why cultural minorities were not receiving appropriate treatment and includes a special section on preventive services. The ensuing legislation recommended by President Carter, which was supposed to increase the responsiveness of community mental health centers to the needs of minorities, was entitled the Mental Health Systems Act of 1980. Wagenfeld and Jacobs have outlined its major themes:

> continued support of the CMHC program, authorization of grants for programs providing both mental health and related support services for three highly vulnerable groups of mentally ill persons (the chronically mentally ill, severely disturbed children and adolescents, and elderly persons); and flexible new opportunities for the most needy areas to receive federal support for programs providing a core set of community-based services for these same high-risk groups or other populations with unmet needs—for example, the urban and rural poor, and ethnic and racial minorities.[27]

The 1980 program was passed, but never enacted due to the efforts of President Reagan. He replaced the 1980 Act with the Omnibus Budget Reconciliation Act of 1981, and thereby introduced the Alcohol and Drug Abuse and Mental Health Block Grant programs.[28] In effect, this maneuver dismantled the federal role in organizing community mental health services. Further, the Block Grant initiative did not mention minorities, and contains only a brief statement that "consultation and education services" should be provided under this program. However, no standards were established for such programs. Accompanying this change in direction was a clear message to the National Institute of Mental Health to refrain from sponsoring projects that were "activist" in orientation, or identified racism and other forms of discrimination or inequality as the basis for research or demonstration projects.

Conceptual and Professional Ambiguities of the Center Movement

Fundamental omissions or ambiguities obfuscated the role of, and created conflicts within, community mental health centers, especially in terms of meeting the mental health needs of minority groups. Most of these are exemplified by the absence of specific language pertaining to minorities. However, the conceptual thinking was also muddled. For example, the term "mental health" covered a broad terrain. Included were manifestations of psychopathology ranging from minor transitory mood disturbances to organic disorders. Accordingly, intervention settings could range from informal social networks in the community to large state hospitals. Even drug and alcohol abuse treatment were within the purview of CMHCs. The imprecision of the term also made difficult the establishment of realistic program parameters or evaluation criteria.

A confounding issue was encountered when outlining service regions. Service areas were supposed to "conform to boundaries of one or more school districts or political or other subdivisions in the State." The primary basis for allocating funds for centers was done on a per-capita basis, and a population range was established (75,000–200,000) for catchment areas that should be served by one center. However, this formula never took into the account the demographic and cultural complexity of a service region. Nor was any consideration given to the fact that such diversity could have implications with regard to minorities having access to proper treatment. Clearly, this was a problem, because many centers had considerable difficulty even attracting a clientele, especially from certain groups such as Hispanics who had no history of utilizing mental health services.[29]

Another related problem pertains to the use of the terms "community" and "community psychiatry." There was simply no common operational definitions for these ideas. The supposition that merely placing either a psychiatrist or a mental health facility in a minority neighborhood would somehow make these practitioners culturally sensitive underscores the poverty of both the theory and research used to guide the community mental health movement. While P.L. 94-63 called for the regular assessment of need and required that up to 2 percent of an agency's funds be spent for evaluating services, this money was rarely used for this purpose or for understanding the needs of minorities. Moreover, formal and informal social networks of minorities are complex and stratified vertically by socioeconomic status and horizontally by cultural orientation.[30] Nevertheless, little progress was made in developing methods for assessing need, mapping social networks, outlining entry procedures for culturally diverse communities, or developing techniques for understanding the mental health beliefs and practices already present in multicultural communities.

This community orientation also brought into focus several sources of role conflict for mental health professionals: to be professionals who are committed to the medical model or social innovators; to offer traditional services via facilities located in the community or become a new hybrid of healer and community organizer. The former views were associated with the traditional role that had official guild sanction, while the latter forced practitioners to abandon familiar theories and methods.

Predictably, many observers railed against the dilution of the "pure" professional role. Dunham noted that a mere listing of all the functions that were now within the auspices of community psychiatry was quite simply overwhelming.[31] He also observed that sociologists may be pleased that psychiatrists had finally discovered the community, but the question was whether the latter had any business there. He did not believe psychiatrists understood the link between socio-environmental factors and psychiatric disorders. This situation made treatment speculative at best, because psychiatrists were not trained in social intervention. In fact, Dunham suggested that if psychiatrists really wanted to go out and work for community change, they should run for public office.

As early as 1969, Sabshin had already classified psychiatrists as following into three major ideologies: psychotherapeutic, somatotherapeutic, and sociotherapeutic.[32] The existence of these camps was, presumably, blocking progress toward the holistic approach advocated by the members of the community mental health movement. A somatotherapist is most likely to conceive of psychiatric disorders as having a biological basis and utilize a somatic treatment. Psychotherapists emphasize psychological, or intrapsychic, models of etiology, and prefer psychotherapy as the treatment of choice. These practitioners believe that specific models of etiology are identifiable, as are precise treatment modalities. On the other hand, the sociotherapist was more likely to favor socio-environmental explanations of psychiatric disorders that put aside specific disease models of mental illness in favor of schemes that take into account social processes. In the end, the so-called sociotherapist was supposed to prevail.

Consequently, many disaffected psychiatrists abandoned the community mental health movement and, in fact, the actual percentage of psychiatrists, as a proportion of all mental health center professional staff, declined. Ultimately the tenuous legitimacy of the community mental health movement was eroded, once programs began to be dominated by social workers. Although the experience was far from universal, the guild rivalry at times resembled class warfare, with corresponding heated conflicts and organizational divisiveness. One of the authors recalls vividly a statewide county mental health directors meeting in California in 1979 where this issue was addressed. During this assembly, the former director of the State Department of Mental Health announced to an audience of several hundred that he had no intentions of "presiding over a war between social workers and psychiatrists refereed by psychologists." Nonetheless, the loss of support from psychiatrists contributed to the declining fortunes of the movement.

Since there were few minority psychiatrists, and many more minority social workers, the attrition of psychiatrists was also a positive development because the presence of minority practitioners among public mental health providers was increased. Though few in number, these minority social workers, along with a few clinical psychologists, were an important source of program innovation, including the development of culture-specific treatment modalities and community outreach programs for the early detection and referral of cases, as well as pioneering efforts in the use of community-based educational interventions.[33]

The Golden Age of Minority Mental Health

Throughout the community mental health movement, the development and application of methodologies for assessing the cultural composition of minority communities and understanding their lifestyles was slowed by the lack of trained mental health professionals, who possessed the ethnographic skills necessary to function appropriately in multicultural-multilingual environments. There were some very important, though rare, exceptions to this charge. Intense national efforts to support the training of minority mental health practitioners, such as the training programs sponsored by the National Institute of Mental Health, were slow to commence, but eventually did produce a small cadre that began to find its way into the community mental health field in the mid-1970s. The Institute also funded a few minority research centers during this period, which, it was hoped, would provide new knowledge that was badly needed for revising the curriculum of mental health training programs, in addition to retraining practitioners who were already in the field. The success of these centers in accomplishing their mission is not absolutely clear, but their existence helped to usher in a more sophisticated perspective concerning the mental health needs, behaviors, and belief systems of minorities. Unfortunately, the minority mental health research centers, along with their federal administrative counterpart, the Minority Center, were isolated and never brought into the mainstream at the National Institute of Mental Health.

However, this progress was relatively short-lived, because of the budget cuts that occurred in the 1980s. As a result of this retrenchment, culturally sensitive outreach interventions and treatment approaches were abandoned, in favor of traditional clinical services. Restrictive payment mechanisms did not improve this situation. Further, the development time was not long enough to produce a critical mass of minority professionals who could move into direct services or policy positions in state agencies, hospitals, and the National Institute of Mental Health, or into university research and teaching.

The political context of the nation, as noted previously, set the stage both for the creation and erosion of the community mental health movement. For example, the community mental health centers were launched during the "Great Society" years of President Johnson. After Johnson left office legislative support was strong enough to guarantee continuing appropriations throughout the 1960s and 1970s, despite serious efforts to end the federal role in community mental health by President Nixon.[34] The Carter presidency and the intense interest in mental health expressed by Roslynn Carter, brought about renewed interest in community mental health. The Carter years could be termed a "mid-course correction" for the community mental health movement, as scholars and practitioners were brought together to assess comprehensively the adequacy of public mental health services and to discuss the research and program innovations that were shown to be effective during the previous fifteen years of experimentation. This process was shortcircuited by the incoming Reagan Administration, which was opposed on ideological grounds to the community mental health movement, apathetic to the problems of minorities, and looking for ways to reduce programs. To paraphrase David Stockman on this point, when he was acting as Reagan's Director of Office of Management and Budget: "Since when is community mental health the business of the federal government?" This was certainly a new juncture in federal sponsorship.

Theoretically, the community mental health movement should have been self-sustaining by this time, despite the fact that less than half of the targeted 2000 community mental health centers were ever constructed. However, a drop in federal support and leadership occurred at the same time as many state-level budget crises. These state shortages soon became endemic, as a direct result of tax reform and a reluctance to impose new taxes to support social services. Moreover, there was also a short-fall in third-party payment revenues, which were supposed to cover a considerable portion of treatment costs. The community mental health movement simply could not be sustained in the face of diminishing resources and increasing service demands. Additionally, mental health agencies were now in head-to-head competition with other human services providers for state general funds.

The Block Grant Program provided for less federal control and red tape, as a result of allowing each state to determine the level of mental health services it was willing to sustain. Since these changes were occurring at the very same time that mental hospitals were closing, thereby returning mental patients en masse to "community treatment," the result was to transform CMHCs into care centers for chronic patients. This development has significantly directed staff resources away from other target populations and services and toward maintenance therapy for psychotic clients. Actually, this latter patient population was supposed to have been a primary target of CMHCs since their inception. In practice, however, mixing formerly hospitalized patients with subacute nonchronic patients is difficult to accomplish, particularly without proper funding.

In response to intense deinstitutionalization efforts, states have rushed to create "continuum of care" models and operating standards, in an effort to unite existing services and providers into a coordinated treatment system. Within this framework case managers ride herd on nonhospitalized, chronic patients. Nevertheless, the fiscal impact on state community mental health systems has been staggering. California, which was a pioneer state in the community mental health system, has had to cut services so drastically that only modalities intended for chronically mentally ill adults and disturbed children remain in many counties. This is a far cry from the 1975 version of the Community Mental Health Centers Act, which obligated centers, perhaps unrealistically, to provide twelve services. Furthermore, quite often case managers have so many active cases that there is little hope of client supervision.

Prevention Theory and Practice

The community mental health model included prevention services. Due to this emphasis on experimentation, early intervention became one of the important services directed to minorities. Yet the first casualties of the federal recisions and Block Grant Program were outreach and community education programs. After 1981, because such programs could not be reimbursed by any payment mechanism, they quickly evaporated.

Prevention is consistently mentioned in discussions about the philosophical and theoretical rationale for community-based facilities, as well as the authorizing legislation that was enacted throughout the history of the community mental health movement. Furthermore, starting with the Presidential Commission on Mental Health in 1978, a strong initiative was begun in order to fund prevention research centers and community trials at the National Institute of Mental Health, as well as to encourage individual states to create prevention offices in their respective state mental health agencies. In point of fact, the Task Panel Report of the President's Commission called for a paradigm shift toward primary prevention. The underlying rationale for this shift was the acceptance of a basic socio-environmental axiom: "The critical point is that while all behavior has an underlying physiological basis, disturbed behavior need not imply an underlying pathological organic process."[35] Stated differently, searching for a single cause for every disorder is futile, because many environmental stressors are involved in precipitating a psychiatric event. Advanced by the Task Panel was a program of primary prevention aimed at high-risk groups that strengthened their coping resources and which relied on educational interventions rather than therapy. With regard to existing services, the most important point was that emphasis should be shifted from remediation to the prevention of mental health problems.

With the advent of the Block Grant Program, the National Institute of Mental Health was left in the position of funding community trials of prevention models that had no hope of being implemented at the community level. This is because the justification for federal innovation and information dissemination implicit in the Community Mental Health Centers Act of 1963 was no longer operative. This development, combined with the restrictions on payment mechanisms for prevention, brought an untimely end to the prevention era in mental health. Many of the same arguments assembled by the psychiatric establishment to undermine the community mental health movement were also marshalled against the new wave of prevention trials. In short, these experiments were held to be premature in the absence of etiological models for specific disorders.[36] Curiously, as noted in the Task Force Report, this standard is not operative in justifying traditional somatic or psychodynamic therapies for mental disorders; nor is it required in public health epidemiology. In fact, presumably because the value of traditional therapies is not in question, controlled outcome studies of traditional treatment modalities are rare.

Persistent Problems in Meeting Minority Needs

Although the community mental health movement was intended to help all who needed mental health care, this orientation was potentially an especially important source of care for cultural minority groups because many of them have no viable treatment alternative. However, from the outset, there is little evidence that mental health practitioners and planners had any grasp of what they were getting themselves into relative to the treatment of these persons. Perhaps the philosophy of the community mental health movement was never fully appreciated by these professionals. After all, they had been trained to adopt a very different set of role expectations. There was no curriculum then, and precious little training now, pertaining to intervention with culturally diverse clients. The formal preparation of psychiatrists and psychologists has rarely included a systematic presentation or discussion of cultural information. Even social workers have had only a slight advantage in terms of appreciating the relevance of culturally based knowledge. Moreover, most practitioners have seldom received any ethnomethodological training. Even after these deficits were widely acknowledged, and significant headway was made in minority research, little has been done to rectify the situation.

In the absence of a knowledge base pertaining to minority mental health within the standard academic curricula, minority mental health practitioners were still perceived as the natural experts on transcultural psychiatry, intervention, and treatment. Some were ready to deal with these expectations by advocating new program ideas and implementing them as well. Some were not. Ironically, since minority professionals received the same formal training as everyone else, often they were intellectually wed to the same guild priorities and traditional therapies that were undermining the implementation of a truly integrated treatment system.[37] Worse still, some minority professionals exhibited airs of superiority, or expressed social class biases, in dealing with members of their own ethnic group. In other instances, insufficient availability of minority professional staff members often led to the hiring of foreign nationals of the same racial or broad linguistic-cultural grouping, in the hope that they, being "generic ethnics," would be more culturally sensitive or acceptable to minority patients. However, this alternative was too often disappointing because these individuals tended to have little knowledge of and did not identify with the target population, in addition to lacking an awareness of local socio-environmental conditions.

Despite a dramatic upsurge in minority mental health research after 1975 inadequate training is still received by both minority and nonminority practitioners.[38] Moreover, university research remains disconnected from the practice of community mental health. This situation results from a lack of formal ties between universities and community mental health providers, which, if corrected, could provide stimulation and guidance for both practitioners and researchers. For example, academics could help to generate new intervention models and test specific theories in minority communities. Fortunately, a few examples are available to illustrate how this marriage of academics and service providers could be accomplished, and some of these have even survived the recent downward spiral of funding. In every instance, however, strong leadership, support, and participation from the community mental health administrators are required to make the relationship productive and enduring.

Ties between universities and mental health providers are also very important for recruiting minority students into the field of community mental health, either as researchers or practitioners. Although public mental health services have been weakened, a new initiative is needed to deal with the demographic realities of urban America. The population growth for Hispanics and Asians, resulting from higher fertility rates and continuing immigration, are compelling. For example, the U.S. Bureau of the Census reported that the Hispanic population in 1987 had reached 18.8 million persons, a net increase of 4.3 million since 1980. Moreover, this figure will increase again before the 1990 census, due to the inclusion of approximately three million individuals legalized under the 1986 Immigration Reform and Control Act and a continuing influx of persons from Mexico and the Caribbean Basin. Asian immigration is also highly complex and dramatically increasing, with 1,347,705 Asians admitted between 1980 and 1985! The demographic composition of the largest cultural minority groups, especially African Americans and Latin Americans, indicates a lower mean age, lower educational attainment, and lower-income levels than non-Hispanic whites.[39] Accordingly, a reasonable assumption is that there will be an increasing need for public and private mental health services for minorities, and that future planning will require far greater sophistication for engaging a wide range of cultural and linguistic groups, with increased emphasis placed on children's services.

Conclusion

A cul de sac has been reached by the community mental health movement. The experimentation that was supposed to take place with regard to service delivery has, for the most part, ended. As is noted throughout this chapter, a host of factors has contributed to the demise of this approach to intervention. The recently burgeoning political conservatism, tension among professionals, inadequate theories and methods, inappropriate training, and a lack of funding all played a role in this failure. Apparently, the early pioneers in community mental health never realized the truly radical implications of their proposals. Delivering services in terms of a philosophy of community-based treatment, shook the foundation of the mental health establishment. Yet the guidance necessary to move ahead in conceptual and practical matters was not available, and thus progress toward culturally equitable services was limited.

Kurt Lewin once said that adequate practice will not occur without good theory. In other words, a conceptual scheme must be formulated that justifies and orients intervention in a community-based manner, if this treatment strategy is to succeed. If increased cultural sensitivity and awareness are assumed to improve intervention, the rationale for this claim must be clearly stated. Otherwise, the philosophy of community mental health may come to be viewed as nothing more than a platitude. The following chapter, therefore, is devoted to discussing the psychological and sociological theories that were prevalent during the early stages of developing community-based intervention. These theories, moreover, are shown to be inadequate for this task. Accordingly, a new conceptual paradigm is suggested, one which encourages the creation of diagnostic methods, intervention strategies, and training modules that are culturally sensitive. In short, a novel approach to conceptualizing knowledge and order that is consistent with the aims of a culturally pluralistic, community-based intervention is offered.

Notes

1. Wells, Kenneth, Jacqueline Golding, Richard Hough, Audrey Burnam, and Marvin Karno. "Acculturation and the Probability of Use of Health Services by Mexican Americans," *Health Services Research* 24(2), 1989, pp. 236–257; Wells, Kenneth, Richard Hough, Jacqueline Golding, Audrey Burnam, and Marvin Karno. "Which Mexican Americans Underutilize Health Services?" *American Journal of Psychiatry* 144(7), 1987, pp. 918–922.

2. Dworkin, Rosalind J. and George L. Adams. "Retention of Hispanics in Public Sector Mental Health Services," *Community Mental Health Journal* 23(3), 1987, pp. 204–216; Humm-Delgado, Denise and Marvin Delgado. "Assessing Hispanic Mental Health Needs: Issues and Recommendations," *Journal of Community Psychology* 11(4), 1983, pp. 363–372; Padilla, Amado M., Rene A. Ruiz, and Rudolpho Alvarez. "Community Mental Health Services for the Spanish-speaking/Surnamed Population," *American Psychologist* 30(9), 1975, pp. 892–905; Sue, Stanley. "Barriers Between Mental Health Services and Mexican Americans: An Examination of Paradox," *American Journal of Community Psychology* 7(5), 1979, pp. 503–520; Sue, Stanley, H. McKinney, D. Allen, and J. Hall. "Delivery of Community Mental Health Service to Black and White Clients," *Journal of Consulting and Clinical Psychology* 42(6), 1974, pp. 794–801; Sue, Stanley and Thom Moore (eds.). *The Pluralistic Society*. (New York: Human Services Press, Inc., 1984).

3. Good, Byron J. and Mary-Jo Good. "The Cultural Context of Diagnosis and Therapy: A View from Medical Anthropology." In *Mental Health Research and Practice in Minority Communities: Development of Culturally Sensitive Training Programs*, ed. Manuel Miranda and Harry Kitano. (Rockville, MD: ADMHA, DHHS Pub No. (ADM) 86–1466, 1986), pp. 1–27.

4. Kleinman, Arthur. *Rethinking Psychiatry*. (New York: The Free Press, 1988).

5. Felix, Robert H. "Community Mental Health: A Federal Perspective," *American Journal of Psychiatry* 121(5), 1964, pp. 428–432; Duhl, Leonard J. "New Directives in Mental Health Planning," *Archives of General Psychiatry* 13(5), 1965, pp. 403–410; Bellak, Leopold and Harvey H. Barton (eds.). *Progress in Community Mental Health*. (New York: Guine and Stratton, 1969); Wagenfeld, Morton O., Paul Levenson, and Blair Justice (eds.). *Public Mental Health*. (Beverly Hills, CA: Sage, 1982).

6. DeRisi, William and William Vega. "The Impact of Deinstitutionalization on California's State Hospital Population," *Hospital and Community Psychiatry* 34(2), 1983, pp. 140–144.

7. Ruben, Bernard. "Community Psychiatry," *Archives of General Psychiatry* 20(5), 1969, pp. 497–507; Rossi, Ascanio M. "Some Pre-World War II Antecedents of Community Mental Health Theory and Practice." In *Perspectives in Community Mental Health*, ed. Arthur J. Bindeman and Allen D. Spiegel. (Chicago: Aldine, 1969), pp. 9–28.

8. Biegel, Allen and Alan I. Levenson. "Mental Health Center: Origins and Concepts." In *The Community Mental Health Center*, ed. Allen Biegel and Alan I. Levenson. (New York: Basic Books, 1972) pp. 3–18.

9. Srole, Leo, Thomas Langner, Stanley Michael, P. Kirkpatrick, Marvin Opler, and Thomas A. Rennie, *Mental Health in the Metropolis: The Midtown Manhattan Study*. (New York: New York Community Press, 1978); Srole, Leo and Anita K. Fisher, "The Midtown Manhattan Longitudinal Study vs. the 'Mental Paradise Lost' Doctrine," *Archives of General Psychiatry* 37(2), 1980, pp. 209–221.

10. Barter, James T. "California—Transformation of Mental Health Care: 1957–1982." In *Unified Health Systems: Utopia Unrealized*, ed. John A. Talbott. (San Francisco: Jossey-Bass, 1983), pp. 7–18.

11. Stretch, John J. "Community Mental Health: The Evolution of a Concept in Social Policy," *Community Mental Health Journal* 3(1), 1967, pp. 5–12.

12. "Mental Illness and Mental Retardation—Message from the President of the United States," *Congressional Record*. (Washington, DC: U.S. Government Printing Office, February 5, 1963), pp. 1837–1842.

13. Zusman, Jack. "Sociology and Mental Illness," *Archives of General Psychiatry* 15, 1966, pp. 635–648; Goffman, Erving. *Asylums*. (Garden City, NY: Doubleday Anchor, 1961); Wing, John K. and George Brown. *Institutionalization and Schizophrenia*. (Cambridge: Cambridge University Press, 1970).

14. Szaz, Thomas S. *The Myth of Mental Illness*. (New York: Harper and Row, 1961).

15. American Public Health Association. *Mental Disorders: A Guide to Control Methods*. (New York: APHA, 1962); Bloom, Bernard L. "Prevention of Mental Disorders: Recent Advances in Theory and Practice," *Community Mental Health Journal* 15(3), 1979, pp. 179–191; Wagenfeld, Morton O. "The Primary Prevention of Mental Illness: A Sociological Perspective," *Journal of Health and Social Behavior* 13(1), 1972, pp. 102–109; Schulberg, Herbert. "State Planning for Community Mental Health Programs: Implications for Psychologists," *Community Mental Health Journal* 1(1), 1965,

pp. 37–42; Caplan, Gerald. *Principles of Preventive Psychiatry*. (New York: Basic Books, 1964).

16. Rodgers, Edward S. "Man, Ecology, and the Control of Disease," *Public Health Reports* 77(9), 1962, pp. 755–762.

17. Faris, Robert E. L. and H. Warren Dunham. *Mental Disorders in Urban Areas*. (Chicago: University of Chicago Press, 1939).

18. Kohn, Melvin L. "Social Class and Schizophrenia: A Critical Review." In *The Transmission of Schizophrenia*, ed. David Rosenthal and Seymour S. Kety. (Oxford: Pergaman Press, 1968), pp. 155–173; Bloom, Bernard. *Changing Patterns of Psychiatric Care*. (New York: Human Sciences Press, 1975); Hollingshead, August B. and Frederick C. Redlich. *Social Class and Mental Illness: A Community Study*. (New York: John Wiley and Sons, 1958).

19. Selye, Hans. *The Stress of Life*. (New York: McGraw Hill, 1956).

20. Gaviria, M. and G. Stern. "Problems in Designing and Implementing Culturally Relevant Mental Health Services for Latinos," *U.S. Social Science and Medicine* 143(1), 1980, pp. 65–71.

21. Newbrough, John R. "Community Mental Health: A Movement in Search of a Theory." In *Perspectives in Community Mental Health*, ed. Arthur J. Bindman and Allen D. Spiegel. (Chicago: Aldine, 1969), pp. 70–78.

22. Feldman, Saul. "Promises, Promises or Community Mental Health Services Training: Ships That Pass in the Night," *Community Mental Health Journal* 14(2), 1978, pp. 83–91.

23. Leeds, Alice, Jon Gudemon, Kent Miller, and Alan I. Levenson. "Planning for Mental Health Care," *Community Mental Health Journal* 5(3), 1969, pp. 206–214.

24. Mayo, Julia C. "What is the Social in Social Psychiatry?" *Archives of General Psychiatry* 14(5), 1966, pp. 449–455.

25. Public Law 94-63. Title III—Community Mental Health Care. USC 2689. (Washington, DC: U.S. Government Printing Office, July 29, 1975), 89 STAT 308–346.

26. *President's Commission on Mental Health*. (Washington, DC: U.S. Government Printing Office, 1978).

27. Wagenfeld, "Community Mental Health Movement," p. 65. In *Public Mental Health*, ed. Wagenfeld, Levinson, and Justice.

28. Public Law 979–35. Omnibus Budget Reconciliation Act of 1981 (USC 1331). (Washington, DC: U.S. Government Printing Office, August 13, 1981), 95 STAT 357–604.

29. Torrey, E. Fuller. "The Case for the Indigenous Therapist," *Archives of General Psychiatry* 20(3), 1969, pp. 365–373.

30. Gordon, Milton. *Assimilation in American Life*. (New York: Oxford Press, 1964).

31. Dunham, A. Warren. "Community Psychiatry," *Archives of General Psychiatry* 12(3), 1965, pp. 303–313.

32. Sabshin, Melvin. "The Anti-Community Mental Health 'Movement,' " *American Journal of Psychiatry* 125(8), 1969, pp. 41–47.

33. Comas-Diaz, Lillian and Ezra E. H. Griffith. *Clinical Guidelines in Cross-Cultural Mental Health*. (New York: John Wiley and Sons, 1988).

34. Bench Notes. "ADAMHA's Emerging Role in the Block Grants Program," *The Journal of NIH Research*, 1(3), 1989, p. 124.

35. Presidential Commission on Mental Health, "Report of the Task Panel on Prevention." (Washington, DC: U.S. Government Printing Office, February 15, 1978), pp. 1822–1863.

36. Lamb, H. Richard and Jack Zusman. "Primary Prevention in Perspective," *American Journal of Psychiatry* 136(1), 1979, pp. 2–17.

37. Lefley, Harriet P. "Delivering Mental Health Services Across Cultures." In *Mental Health Services: The Cross-Cultural Context*, ed. Paul B. Pedersen, Norman Sarborius, and Anthony J. Marsella. (Beverly Hills, CA: Sage, 1984), pp. 135–171.

38. Newton, Frank Cota-Robles, Esteban L. Olmedo, and Amado M. Padilla. *Hispanic Mental Health Research, A Reference Guide*. (Berkeley, CA: University of California Press, 1982).

39. Bean, Frank and Marta Tienda. *The Hispanic Population of the United States*. (New York: Russell Sage Foundation, 1987).

Chapter Two

Theory Development in the Early Days

Introduction

As is noted in chapter one, the delivery of social services was supposed to be altered significantly subsequent to the passage of the Community Mental Health Centers Act. Clients were to be treated in the "least restrictive environment," while "citizen participation" in the planning and provision of services was to be encouraged.[1] Contrary to the state hospital model, the focus of intervention should be the community. An appropriate level of community involvement for a client should be ascertained. Likewise, treatment planning should be integrated and comprehensive. What this means is that a wide range of persons should be involved with clients, rather than simply medical personnel. Treatment, in other words, was changed from primarily a medical to a social undertaking. No longer should the interaction that takes place between clients and therapists be guided by socially insensitive criteria.

Considering the many attempts that have been made to identify mental illness, advancing a comprehensive definition of this phenomenon would be foolhardy at this juncture. Nonetheless a few remarks are in order, particularly with regard to appreciating the thrust of a community-based orientation.

Traditionally terms and phrases such as "defect of reason," "inability to understand," "malfunction," "impairment," and "lack of sound judgment" have been used to describe mental illness.[2] Community-based practitioners are supposed to recognize that these ideas, along with the so-called "markers" of health and illness, do not exist in a vacuum. When talking about reason, for example, assumptions are made about the appropriateness of behavior. Therefore, isolating and cataloging these identifiers became very problematic. Simply put, a variety of critics began to doubt whether discrete categories could ever be procured for this purpose.[3] Defied by the idea of community mental health, in other words, is the simple classification of individual psychological events.

This shift in logistics was precipitated by a new philosophy. In short, the knowledge base used to make decisions should be community-based. Diagnoses and treatment recommendations should incorporate important cultural considerations, rather than arcane psychiatric standards. Biomedical explanations of illness, accordingly, are to be tempered by socio-environmental factors. The search for the causes of problems should not be limited to a particular realm. In fact, a pluralistic approach to treatment is supposed to be fostered. Instead of restricted, the knowledge base of practitioners should be flexible and permitted to expand as far as possible. Hence innovation and experimentation were elevated in importance.

As opposed to the medical model, treatment standardization was not supposed to be a highly valued principle. Indeed, the sort of value-freedom that is associated with the disease concept may render clinical judgments irrelevant. Because explanations of illness were now understood to be united inextricably to differences in language use, cultural themes, and a plethora of social variables, treatment should be value-based. However, under the guise of value-freedom and science, these so-called subjective elements are often viewed by traditional mental health practitioners and researchers as impeding the development of sound intervention strategies. Precision, accordingly, has tended to be equated with methodological or procedural rigor. Yet when rigor is pursued as a panacea, precise but socially insensitive clinical judgments are likely to follow. As summarized nicely by Eysenck, "atheoretical" classificatory schemes are "empty" and "unreliable."[4]

As is suggested, the Community Mental Health Centers Act is underpinned explicitly by the belief that intervention should be guided by the principle of social sensitivity.[5] The values that pervade a community should be thought of as relevant to the acquisition of clear and concise knowledge about behavior and cultural beliefs. In more concrete terms, input from community members should not be understood to compromise the decision making process of planners in designing interventions and proposing didactic therapies. Clients should be envisioned to be involved actively in both securing and evaluating treatment. At this juncture an important point must be emphasized: the values, beliefs, and commitments exhibited by citizens should not be treated as ancillary to scientific concepts, but should be understood to play a prime role in differentiating health from illness. Stated differently, the so-called human element should extend to the core of the intervention process.

Clearly this epistemology elevates in importance cultural factors in distinguishing illness behavior. Minorities, accordingly, can only benefit from this shift in thinking. Cultural norms concerning issues such as tolerance of symptoms, responsibility for care, use of medication, or personal beliefs about illness no longer have to be viewed as anathema to prescribing a sound treatment regimen. The cultural context of a problem should not be an impediment to making an accurate diagnosis, subsequent to accepting the philosophy of community-based intervention.

Paradoxically, placing the stock of knowledge used by persons to regulate their lives at the center of intervention activities represents a kind of heresy.[6] After all, scientists are expected to be unimpressed by opinions. Through the use of a variety of methodological techniques, such as rigid clinical protocols, interpretation of cultural information and other human foibles are assumed to be moved to the periphery of any investigation. In this sense, diagnostic judgments are rendered on the basis of a narrow conception about the facts of a case. But are facts this obtrusive or objective? According to many advocates of community mental health the answer should be no. Knowledge is not pristine, but associated directly with social interests.[7] What this means with regard to clinical practice is that an abstract nomenclature may mask socially constructed definitions of reality. And as a result, the social significance of behavior may be overlooked. For example, mental illness may be viewed as nothing more than the absence of reason. A misguided diagnosis such as this is encouraged when clinical judgments are not grounded thoroughly in local culture.

Knowledge and Dualism

Putting this much faith in procedural rigor is justified by paradoxical thinking. That is, using formal diagnostic protocol calls for inserting procedural distance between a researcher and whatever is known. This, in turn, is assumed to result in the acquisition of valid knowledge. This viewpoint is sustained by the claim that subjectivity and objectivity should be kept separate, if sound clinical decisions are to be made. For this reason, a lot of time and effort has been devoted to improving diagnostic nosologies. Therefore, subjectivity or opinion cannot defile a format that will insure that sound and consistent diagnoses are rendered by practitioners. The implicit logic of adhering closely to technical parameters is that the contaminating effects of interpretation will be purged from intervention.[8] Adhering to stepwise instructions, it is argued, does not require any commentary. Diagnoses will thus not be clouded by extraneous considerations.

Is this a valid conception of knowledge? Apparently even the creators of the DSM-III (Diagnostic and Statistical Manual, 3rd Edition) wanted to abandon this rarefied epistemology, for they were aware of the impact culture has on identifying a problem. But because no real cultural axis exists, introducing this factor is left to the discretion and knowledge of the individual therapist. Moreover, the extreme formalization of decision making that accompanies the DSM-III discourages the development of cultural sensitivity. The issue of cultural awareness, therefore, is not really taken seriously.

As Michel Foucault writes, clients are approached as ideal persons, who do not have a unique biography.[9] In this sense, health and illness are conceptualized as if these ideas do not have any relationship to social existence. Jacques Derrida describes this outcome when he states that traditionally clients have been crushed under the mode of reasoning adopted by psychologists and psychiatrists.[10] How can accuracy be forthcoming from such insensitivity? Most likely all that will happen is the behavior of clients will be misconstrued. Likewise, the community will not be treated as an appropriate location to inaugurate intervention activities, because anything that is remotely associated with subjectivity, or lacks a formal protocol, must be eschewed.

Traditionally any process that pertains to the acquisition of objective knowledge must be neutralized. This thesis is basically dualistic. On the one hand objectivity is recognized, while on the other interpretation blocks access to this information. As long as this distinction can be maintained, a knowledge base that is reliable is thought to be available. In fact, diagnostic nosologies, medically inspired models of illness, and laboratory protocol perform this function. These prosthetic aids, as postmodernists call them, are adopted to reinforce perception and avoid judgments that are flawed by human errors.[11] That is, technical procedures are used to collect information and render decisions. The problem is that an extremely sterile image of social life is proffered. Moreover, this imagery is inconsistent with a key theme of community mental health. Specifically, the perceptions of patients and clients are not allowed to contribute appreciably to the accumulation of clinical knowledge.

Accompanying this dualistic view of a clinical knowledge base is the reification of the social world. As recommended by Emile Durkheim, facts are treated as objects or things.[12] In other words, the meaning of an event is believed to be derived from its empirical properties. Natural laws, accordingly, are understood to give the impetus to behavior. As might be suspected, social intervention is presumed to be similar to any other foray into the natural world, for nature and society are envisioned to be identical in many respects. Accordingly, mental illness is just another natural phenomenon. In line with the medical model, natural causes are thought to have physiological impact, which, in turn, culminates in abnormal behavior.[13] Clinicians who utilize the proper techniques are assumed to be capable of identifying facts on the basis of their empirical traits. Key to success in this endeavor is technical competence, whereby value-free procedures are invoked to generate valid evidence. The link between natural causes and behavior, therefore, can be isolated and rendered explicit.

But what about the human element? Surely mental illness is embedded within a social context. Almost by definition empirically derived information is insufficient to classify deviant acts. These data are simply empirical, while deviance implies the presence of value judgments. As a result, claiming that objective facts are indicative of behavior can be very misleading.

In more sociological terms, social indicators do not necessarily supply any insight into the causes of behavior. *A* does not strictly lead to *B*, because these or any other social factors are complex processes that do not exist in a vacuum. Variables such as these are mediated by the human presence, because human action cannot be separated neatly from knowledge. However, when the attempt is made to conceptualize social life dualistically, roles, norms, and laws gain a sense of autonomy. These structural factors are not only thought to cause behavior, but serve as a referent for judging normativeness. All cultures, in short, are thought to be underpinned by similar social or psychological laws. Consequently, inanimate objects are the focus of attention during intervention activities.

Suggested in the previous paragraph, however, is that this *modus operandi* is insufficient, particularly in terms of a philosophy that stresses community involvement. Data, behavior, and norms, for example, are not neutral indicators. Instead, these and other components of social life have a human texture, which is inscribed by a host of interpretive elements. To paraphrase G.H. Mead and Herbert Blumer, persons do not react to facts but to their *meaning*.[14] By this they mean behavior is not something that can be assessed accurately by consulting merely its objective properties. Because the meaning of behavior is interpretive, identifying a social problem is much more difficult than is revealed by the medical model. In short, failure to penetrate the interpretive fabric of data can result in the mindless collection of empirical facts that have little relevance to making a socially appropriate diagnosis.

In order for socially sensitive intervention to become commonplace, Kleinman and others state that this démarche must be theoretically justified.[15] They do not doubt that this strategy is warranted, but that the rationale for this change in approach has been sketchy. What is needed is a nondualistic rendition of knowledge and order that can be used to supply the details about how community-based intervention should proceed. Readers must be convinced that purely empirical models of clinical practice are ineffectual, in that they are predicated on faulty premises. For if dualism is legitimate, abandoning the medical model would be foolish! However, if empirical events are inundated by human action, ignoring how social reality is shaped by this source of creativity would make no sense. If the categories of health and illness are socially manufactured, this process should be recognized throughout an intervention.

Several key problems are brought about by dualism that should be summarized at this juncture. First, reality is touted to be objective, or empirical, and thus a reservoir of facts. Second, subjectivity contributes nothing to the survival of this knowledge. Actually, subjectivity is considered to be illogical, irrational, and, in general, something that can sabotage the search for truth. And third, because methods that are empirically based are presumed to be value-free, the use of these techniques is thought to enhance the prospects for gathering factual knowledge. In other words, truth is accessible to those who are technically competent and minimize the effects of interpretation. Obviously these points contradict the spirit of community mental health policies and practices. If these views are accepted, the role played by community sentiment in social planning will certainly be truncated. In the face of obtrusive facts, opinion should pale by comparison. Hence cultural predispositions will likely be subordinated to the opinions expressed by medical experts.

Knowledge and Community-Based Intervention

If community-based intervention is going to have a chance to succeed, new social imagery must be advanced. Having human action intertwined with facts should no longer be treated as unfortunate. Similarly, developing rapport with community members should not be viewed as possibly undermining a needs assessment or any other aspect of intervention. For unless this nondualistic outlook is adopted, the efforts of planners and clinicians may be condemned to irrelevance. In this regard, a useful example can be drawn from the social sciences. "Grand theory," as argued by C. Wright Mills, may be comprehensive but does not have much utility.[16] Empiricists and similar theorists make an identical faux pas, when they demand that valid knowledge must be sequestered from interpretation.

Attaining the status of a positive science, however, requires the acceptance of dualism.[17] Including knowledge in a decision making process that is not clearly empirical and corroborated by laboratory tests, clinical instruments, or another unbiased procedure, is understood to be a mistake. And who wants to be labelled unscientific? Some writers even go so far as to claim that program evaluation data and other planning material are seriously underutilized because they are not scientific.[18] Applied social science, in other words, has not been sufficiently formalized. And until this occurs, clinical practice will also be nothing more than a pseudoscience. The way social scientists have conceptualized reality traditionally testifies to their desire to reveal truth that is unencumbered by opinion. Typically reality or society is portrayed to be an ominous force that is untrammeled by interpretation.[19] Likewise, mental illness is believed to be a natural phenomenon that eventually will be explained. But unless the shortcomings of removing interpretation from intervention are recognized, progress in the development of interventions that are community-based will not be witnessed. The current tendency to medicalize social events will continue unabated, and the interpretive side of illness will remain obscured.

Many authorities did not realize the extent of the demands that community mental health would make on traditional social science. Particularly important is that the theory available during the late 1950s and early 1960s, not to mention most of the views that are prominent today, could not supply the social imagery necessary for this style of intervention to be undertaken on a large scale. Consistent with the desire to be scientific, structural metaphors were used predominately to describe the operation of society. Remember that if society is treated as an inanimate object, dualistic research and intervention methodologies are entirely justified.

So long as norms, health, and deviance, for example, are imagined to be unquestioningly uniform and objective, the need to consult human action to link these factors to social processes will not be seen as urgent. Similarly, extrapolations made on the basis of social indicators will be considered sufficient for planning social services. Overlooked, however, are the *social meaning* of human action, the cultural basis of behavior, the pathways followed to treatment, and the expectations clients have about their problems and therapy. Clearly intervention is not simply a logistical but a social undertaking. This is particularly the case subsequent to the onset of community-based intervention.

Theory and Traditional Intervention

Suggested thus far is that the promises associated with the community mental health movement have not been fulfilled. Although many reasons can be cited for this failure, a theory to justify this kind of intervention is conspicuously absent. In fact, little mention is made of social or psychological theory in the literature that describes community-based treatment. Without the orientation that can be provided by a compatible theory, the rationale for jettisoning the medical model is not explicitly clear. As a result, many of the principles that were operative in state hospitals were simply transferred to community mental health centers. Additionally, when new procedures were proposed, their implementation was often frenetic.[20] Usually intervention was no more relevant, but merely decentralized.

During the late 1950s change was occurring in the United States concerning the status of knowledge. Certainly science was elevated in importance, yet the significance of multidisciplinary approaches was also recognized. This is especially true in the 1960s. Nonetheless, general theories of knowledge and order that are consistent with the thrust of community intervention were not widely discussed. This omission constitutes a major shortcoming. Perhaps it was simply assumed that this sort of perspective would emerge naturally; that such a theory would be a product of the *Zeitgeist*. In any case, the necessary theoretical developments never emerged, and the prevailing mainstream theories did not offer any support for this change in evaluating mental status. Oppositional viewpoints, when they did appear, were not refined sufficiently so that they could be accepted as viable alternatives. In the absence of supporting theory, community-based intervention was handicapped from the start.

Overwhelmingly the psychological and sociological theories that were available are dualistic. This is not to say the models that were invented were not more expansive than in the past. Certainly more factors were cited as possibly affecting a person's mental health. However, simply increasing the number of variables assessed does not necessarily result in social sensitivity. More irrelevant issues, in other words, may be discussed. For this reason, advocates of community intervention should not merely request that more items be added to a traditionally conceived knowledge base. Instead, a specific outlook must be adopted so that the *range* of acceptable knowledge is expanded, thereby promoting the view that definitions of reality are as important as reality. Jacques Lacan captures this sentiment when he argues that truth should be understood to emerge from language and not reality.[21]

His point is that knowledge is not static, when language is understood to mediate reality. Accordingly, social or psychological reality is not associated with unchanging referents. In terms of intervention, this means that the conceptual side of reality should be the focus of attention, rather than the image of knowledge portrayed by science.

Yet in terms of the dominant theories of the time this awareness was not promoted. Instead, valid knowledge was imagined to be fundamentally causal. As noted by David Ingleby, either "strong" or "weak" causal frameworks were advanced.[22] With respect to the former, physiological factors are believed to instigate mental illness. While this approach was tempered somewhat, genetic studies were undertaken regularly in the hope of discovering sound explanations for schizophrenia, alcoholism, and other maladies. By the way, funding for this kind of research has increased in recent years.

On the other hand, sociological considerations were given some attention. In the "weak" sense of causality, environmental factors were thought to join forces with biological ones to create adaptation problems. Again, however, knowledge is not mediated by the human presence. The focus of attention is the objective character of the variables that are reviewed, rather than the "lived world" of persons.[23] The idea that *A* must be interpreted before it leads to *B* or anything else was ignored.

As a consequence of dismissing the modes of reason persons use everyday to explain events, traditional social and psychological theories have stressed the "normalization" of behavior. What this means is that a host of psychological or sociological principles are introduced either overtly or covertly to explain the actions of an individual. Moreover, interventions are inaugurated regularly in accordance with these underlying themes. For example, diagnoses are often based on a form of reason that has been reified for quite some time, and thus has little sound relevance.

Sociological Realism

During the years preceding and for some time after the enactment of the Community Mental Health Act, two sociological theories dominated the intellectual scene. These are functionalism and cybernetics. Theories such as these were deemed acceptable because of their comprehensive nature. A holistic or macro view of society, in other words, was believed to be provided in each case.[24] Nonetheless, this was accomplished through the adoption of a dualistic model. As a result of conceptualizing society to be an anonymous system, a variety of elements could be integrated neatly as never before. Yet this mode of integration is problematic, especially in terms of the mandate to provide social services that are community-based. In short, functionalism and cybernetics are both overtly realistic.

What this means is that human action is not trusted to serve as the foundation of order. The knowledge associated with interpretation is not considered to be substantial enough to regulate society. Talcott Parsons, for example, solved the problem of order by arguing that persons can be linked together structurally.[25] In this regard, he is following the lead of Comte, Spencer, and Durkheim. Parsons made famous the idea of the role and, correspondingly, the role network. In his opinion, role linkages and interaction can be viewed as synonymous, without any undesirable consequence. Specifically, emphasizing the operation of roles does not necessarily obfuscate social dynamics.

Most relevant is that the locus of order is externalized; role prescriptions serve to orient persons. Roles, moreover, are linked by reciprocal expectations, which results in what he calls double contingency. Rather than existing in isolation, roles are complementary. Nurse and doctor, for example, fit together in terms of their functions, thereby insuring the survival of the medical institution. If a person performs his or her role adequately, the maintenance of order is guaranteed. Because the expectations of roles are complementary, the result of fulfilling the requirements of one role is that a person is automatically in synchrony with a host of other roles. Hence order is not dependent on interpretation.

In the mid-1960s, Parsons set out to improve this scheme by supplementing it through the use of cybernetics.[26] Influenced by Norbert Wiener, Parsons accepted the thesis that systems high in energy are subordinate to those which are high in information. Without the orientation supplied by information, in other words, energy would be directionless. As might be suspected, roles supply information, while human action is understood to be merely a source of energy. This means that human action is completely eviscerated, for energy is dominated by information.

What is the importance of these theories for intervention? Roles are independent variables and thus are assumed to shape behavior. Accordingly, the indicators that are associated with roles are believed to provide valuable insight into a person's motives. "Role-strain," for example, produces deviance. Therefore, roles rather than human action are consulted when the guidelines for intervention are formulated. In point of fact, a variety of critics have suggested recently the DSM-III is structured according to conceptual schemes that are believed to be universal and mimic social reality.[27] Standard role expectations, in short, appear to be supplying the rationale for classifying behavior in each case.[28]

Various viewpoints arose to challenge the position advanced by Parsons. A key competitor was symbolic interactionism. Although Herbert Blumer claims he coined this neologism circa 1937, symbolic interactionism did not gain appreciable notoriety until the early to mid-1960s.[29] In opposition to functionalists, symbolic interactionists declare that reality is symbolic. Linguistic habits, in other words, are the harbingers of social reality. True to their pragmatist heritage, symbolic interactionists identify human action as central to understanding the self, norms, and social behavior. Through the creativity unleashed by interaction, reality is constituted and continuously modified. This means human action is an independent variable, instead of the role.

But there is equivocation about the commitment of symbolic interactionists to nondualism, which eventually brings this theory into conflict with community-based intervention. Basically, Blumer and Mead make statements that temper the influence of human action.[30] For example, a distinction is made between natural and social symbols, and symbolic and nonsymbolic interaction. Maintaining these differentiations would be bad enough, but Mead also retains a view of language that is dualistic. He writes that language merely "points to" reality and therefore serves to select possibilities that are assumed to exist.[31] In this respect, language is nothing more than a surrogate for a much more profound phenomenon. Therefore, language does not extend to the core of reality. Reality is the object of language use, and, as Derrida remarks, speech is made to "defer to" reality.[32]

This dualism is manifested in several ways. First, the distinction between a real and social self is retained. Second, as a result of this bifurcation, the attempt has been made regularly to merge language and structure. In some instances the role has been resurrected, but in a linguistic form. When this is the case, language is permitted to alter roles slightly, but subjectivity is never allowed to challenge objectivity seriously.

This dualism is inconsistent with a model of health that is grounded in the community. Reality is supplemented and not necessarily sustained by language. For example, dualism is apparent in the labeling or "social reaction" theory of deviance, which is an outgrowth of symbolic interactionism.[33] The major contribution of this approach is that the focus is ostensibly shifted away from the characteristics of deviants toward those who label these individuals as deviant. Those who apply and enforce labels are recognized as having the ability to force persons into deviant "careers." The key idea is that no behavior is inherently abnormal, and that deviance is socially manufactured. Elevating in importance the relationship between labels and deviance is consistent with the goals of community-based intervention. Yet upon close examination, labels do not really differentiate deviance from normalcy. Specifically, the labeling process constitutes a *reaction* to behavior and thereby does not define the nature of actions. Understanding how labelling occurs merely supplies some insight into the response of a society to a particular behavior.

While this information may be important for analyzing possible barriers to intervention, attention is deflected away from the definitions that create reality. A negative reaction to an issue, such as drug abuse or AIDS, may impede the research and other developments that are essential to providing adequate treatment. Nonetheless, the status of deviant behavior is not critically evaluated. Having a predisposition to act in a particular manner and socially creating reality are not necessarily similar! Presupposed by a reaction is that the stimulus is autonomous, or self-contained. Instead of outlining the reality of behavior, language use merely describes how persons react to a phenomenon. These appraisals, however, are still based on indisputable facts. Labels, in other words, are justified by external referents. Therefore, how the fundamental identity of a behavior is socially created is missed. Clearly, the actual reasoning a client uses to explain illness is obscured, if language is treated as if it simply recapitulates the rules of behavior. At best, the experiential or definitional side of problem identification can be nothing more than an afterthought.

At the same time, numerous renditions of conflict theory were also prevalent.[34] Most of these approaches were influenced by Marx. As a result, the material conditions that are believed to shape social life were given primacy. Again, the aim was to de-emphasize biological, psychological, and other inherent traits in the generation of deviance. Social class and related economic factors were cited to be crucial in the appearance of mental illness and other problems. In actual practice this meant that deviance was assumed to be a product of certain environmental causes, in combination with the ideologies perpetrated by those who have power. As with functionalism, social indicator analysis became very popular. Census tract information, for example, was used extensively to locate environmental situations where deviance is likely to occur. Moreover, economic considerations and biases exhibited by police and other officers of the court were thought to culminate in persons from specific geographic locations being overrepresented in hospitals, prisons, and other agencies.

Similar to functionalism and symbolic interactionism, dualism is evidenced in conflict theory. Environmental factors serve as the base of knowledge, while other cultural themes are ancillary to these objective conditions. In Marxist terms, the base dominates the superstructure. Attention is directed primarily to the context of behavior, because this material realm contains the independent variables. The causes of deviance are thus objectified, while interpretation is dismissed as idealistic. That material factors may be mediated by human action, or praxis, was not yet a popular view to hold. Idealism and materialism were still widely assumed to be irreconcilable. In fact, consciousness was thought by many advocates of conflict theory to prevent the accurate perception of the material laws that are responsible for social problems. The ways in which human action may condition the environment were treated as illusory.

This is not to say that other, less dualistic theories did not exist. Some of these viewpoints will be discussed later in this chapter, under the general heading of postmodern philosophies.[35] During the period when sentiment was building for community mental health, however, these theories were peripheral to social science because of their European ancestry, difficult philosophical orientation, and alleged microlevel of conceptualization. Yet nowadays anti-dualism has achieved a modicum of respectability among many writers and can be employed to legitimize community-based interventions.

Psychological Realism

Psychology was and remains heavily influenced by physiology.[36] Genetic explanations are still sought for everything from drug abuse to schizophrenia. If these pathologies could be understood to progress in a manner similar to other organic problems, such as heart disease, treatment would be relatively easy. Medicine and other physiologically based interventions could be prescribed. In some circles, progress is thought to have been made in this area. Yet defining risk in terms of brain chemistry or similar physiological markers is argued to be reductionistic by a passel of critics, even in terms of understanding common disorders such as mood disturbances, phobias, and alcohol and drug abuse.[37] This kind of ahistorical analysis leaves many avenues of explanation untouched. Concentrating on psycho-organic causes, moreover, is anathema to the holistic approach emphasized by advocates of community-based treatment.

But when psychologists decided to take a more social tact to investigating madness, they were not necessarily any less reductionistic. Behaviorism, for example, was very prominent and overly dualistic. Their Cartesian anxiety, or desire to escape the influence of subjectivity, drove behaviorists to treat the patient as a "black box."[38] What they mean is that no assumptions should be made about the inner states of persons. Accordingly, only objective knowledge should be invoked to explain an event. In this way, the myths that relate to human functioning will be shattered, and speculation about inner conditions and psychic conflicts will no longer restrict analysis. Popular approaches such as reality therapy and behavioral modification, for example, were influenced by behaviorism. Furthermore, enthusiasm has been regenerated lately for treatment regimes organized around counter-conditioning, reconditioning, and desensitization.

Behaviorism offered a new opportunity for the introduction of efficient interventions, due to some success related to the treatment of phobias. Nonetheless, the problem is that those who adopted variants of behaviorism were almost obsessed by clarity. This should be no surprise, since interpretation is believed to confound the search for valid knowledge. Anything associated with the black box is supposed to be avoided. With regard to treatment planning, for example, so-called "weasel" terms should be purged from any description of a client's treatment regimen.[39] In other words, language that suggests the presence of values should be transformed into strict behavioristic goals and objectives. Surprisingly, cognitive and behaviorist approaches have been combined. When this has been tried, however, cognitive operations have assumed the form of behavioral indices. As a result, practitioners were no longer stymied by searching for the ultimate causes of a problem. Something more pragmatic could be undertaken—the desired changes in overt behavior could be inaugurated and monitored. Assumed is that behavioral change is well within the control of clients and is not a product of speculative factors.

Certainly giving legitimacy to social-behavioral analysis is justifiable and laudable. Nonetheless, the way this has been done by behaviorists and neobehaviorists is not necessarily progressive. Referring to persons as black boxes is their most drastic error. Not only are values dismissed as unimportant, interpretation is altogether destroyed as a source of knowledge. Because the experiences that bind a community together have to be operationalized in strictly empirical terms, a trade-off was made, therefore, between expediency and gaining entrée to the actual processes that are at the heart of social life. Accordingly, the "mundane reason" that Pollner claims sustains order is translated into easily measurable criteria.[40] Most troublesome about this practice is that the cultural side of illness is diminished in importance.

As a way of overcoming the rigidity imposed by behaviorism, Freudian theory became quite popular. Of course, this was not traditional psychotherapy. The move to outpatient treatment required that "briefer" approaches to analysis had to be invented.[41] Prowling around the depths of a person's psyche for years no longer seemed to be an efficient mode of intervention. Therefore, depth psychology was significantly modified. The guiding question became, what type of changes could be affected in a limited number of counseling sessions? In order to answer this query, the social side of Freudian analysis was resurrected. "Present-centered" problems, in other words, should be remedied with pragmatic solutions. Perhaps the interpersonal dynamics that are instrumental in causing psychic trauma could be addressed? Therefore, training could be provided whereby clients learn to better manage their environments. As might be expected, attention was directed to the family and other locations of primary group relationships. In short, emphasized by briefer psychotherapies are coping strategies that enable clients to deal with problematic situations.

But the variant of Freudianism that was adopted is as dualistic as the original. The idea of coping, stated differently, presupposes the presence of an intractable reality.[42] Consequently, persons must learn to accept their lack of freedom as a necessary evil. By implication, the structures imposed by the family and other institutions are accepted as factors that must be effectively managed. Those who cannot cope with the conflicts and ambiguities present in intimate social relationships are bound to suffer discomfort. Whereas in traditional analysis the psychology of these inconsistencies is addressed, in the briefer approaches the social conditions that spawn these difficulties are of prime importance. In either case, however, natural causes are presumed to affect behavior.

Clearly the aim of the briefer psychotherapies is consistent with community-based intervention. Instead of unraveling the secrets of the psyche, contingencies that can be addressed are elevated in importance. Subsequent to the work of Bandura and others, especially Lazarus, "perceived efficacy" and "coping" have become very visible phrases.[43] While these notions are unrelated to psychotherapy per se, a key idea is shared with the "briefer" therapeutic strategies. Put simply, as a result of managing competently their everyday affairs, the mental health of persons is thought to improve. When persons begin to feel they can cope with environmental demands, stress begins to abate and higher esteem results. As should be noted, most important is the appraisal process that accompanies the interaction between persons and their environment. Yet the environment is often portrayed to be a natural context by those who use Freudian theory or the work of Bandura and Lazarus to justify intervention.

Accordingly, the life events or stressors that are likely to occur during a normal lifespan are assumed to follow a regular sequence. In a sense, a kind of Lebensphilosophie appears to be in operation.[44] Coping skills are thus evaluated in terms of how accurately persons perceive their surroundings and select suitable options. As a part of getting away from viewing coping to be a trait, a wide range of responses can be inculcated that will enhance a person's social competence. From a community-based perspective, however, the causal framework that is presupposed is wrong. The criteria for determining successful coping are not an outgrowth of structural necessity but are a product of how persons construct their world. For example, why should the "internal" be considered superior to the "external" locus of control, as appears to be the case in contemporary Western psychology? Since culture is implicated in "coping," as in all other facets of cognitive functioning, no strategy can be considered universal. The fact that an "external" locus of control is more common in Japan does not necessarily render that population incapable of effective coping.

Neither cognitive nor environmental a prioris specify the standards for coping. Instead, personal or culturally based *judgments* provide the referents for evaluating the efficacy of interaction. For example, environmental stressors are culturally defined as part of the appraisal process and are interpreted before coping activity begins. Rather than something loosely referred to as "life events," the assumptions that are made about reality should guide intervention. In this regard, a social network is far more than a context or a coping resource. Instead, a social network consists of the interaction that provides the meaning for understanding events.

So-called "third force" psychology was also available.[45] A few of the writers usually associated with this trend are Ludwig Binswanger, Viktor Frankl, R. D. Laing, Abraham Maslow, Carl Rogers, Thomas Szasz, and so on. The general philosophy espoused by these writers was never taken seriously by community mental health planners. They were thought to be providing social criticism, rather than concrete plans for action. A few exceptions, however, have been witnessed.[46] Due to his interest in the ideas of Laing, Loren Mosher began the Soteria Project. In this undertaking, patients were treated in ordinary houses in residential neighborhoods, rather than in the usual facilities. Another experimental project was undertaken by Paul Polak in Denver, in which the old concept of family care was revived. Most important is that flexibility is stressed in each of these treatment modalities. Medication was rarely used, innovative counseling techniques were created, including goal attainment scaling, and both client and community input were vital to treatment planning. Yet as noted, projects such as these have not been the norm.

Without a clear-cut or consistent theoretical orientation, how could CMHCs be expected to diverge greatly from hospitals? Recent data suggest that the operation of CMHCs is not much different from older institutions, only the scale has changed. A nondualistic epistemology and interpretive social imagery is desperately needed. Accordingly, a comprehensive model for community-based intervention could be formulated, in contrast to the history of ad hoc and piecemeal planning. With the community mental health movement at a standstill, this is the time to consider trying new conceptual schemes. If treatment that is community sensitive is still desired, experimentation is clearly needed. A novel way of conceptualizing knowledge and order may be productive at this juncture.

A Theoretical Justification for Community Intervention

A group of writers, known generally as postmodernists, declare that dualism has always been unjustified. This claim is now given credence in various disciplines, such as philosophy, physics, literary criticism, and theology.[47] The cornerstone of their position is that the human presence cannot be extricated from the knowledge acquisition process. Specifically, postmodernists contend that everything that is known is mediated by language. As they are fond of saying, language games are the source of all knowledge, even the data generated through positive science. Language does not merely point to objects, but shapes whatever is known. According to Jacques Lacan, illness cannot be extricated from symbolism.[48] Objectivity, as defined by Roland Barthes, is simply another modality of signification.[49] In other words, there is no escape from the influence of language. Language penetrates to the core of reality, and thus the usual "metanarratives" pertaining to the pursuit and eventual capture of unadulterated objectivity cannot be sustained.

In terms of understanding norms, truth, or illness, for example, this theoretical shift poses a serious challenge to traditionalists. Any search for these phenomena should take place within the range of "undecidables" indigenous to language. In fact, J. Hillis Miller writes that the search for truth should now be understood as a *mise en abîme*, or an uncertain trek made through the nuances of language.[50] Truth is both revealed through and concealed by layers of interpretation. Facts are not pristine, but can be encountered only indirectly. The aim of acquiring knowledge, accordingly, should be to become familiar with the mode of reason that is operative within the language game of a culture, subculture, or community. Because reality has a linguistic texture, truth should be imagined to stand in the midst of language use.

"Postmodern anthropology," according to a recent commentary, is essential for outlining adequately the criteria that differentiate health from illness.[51] The rationale for this charge is quite simple: only by grasping the intricacies of a definition of reality, can the logic that sustains behavior be grasped. Only by quelling momentarily what Barthes calls "the rustle of language" can knowledge be approached.[52] Clearly this conclusion is consistent with community-based intervention. First, illness reflects the social web within which it resides. Second, diagnoses run the risk of being haphazard unless this realm of interpretation is appreciated. Third, the knowledge base for making clinical judgments is expanded almost indefinitely, for the proliferation of language games does not honor epistemological boundaries that are considered traditionally to be sacrosanct. Interventions, therefore, must adhere to the value base of reality, if the linguistic foundation of a person's world of experience is not to be violated. Actually, according to Jean-Francois Lyotard, a leading postmodernist, disregarding how behavior is interpreted is tantamount to "terrorism."[53] For instance, minority groups that endure the constant insults of a racist society cannot give a favorable assessment to therapy that represents nothing more than cultural imperialism.

As will be shown in later chapters, the nondualism supplied by postmodernism provides unequivocal theoretical justification for community-based interventions. After all, if nothing transcends the effects of language, why would anyone attempt to enter a rarefied domain in order to catch a glimpse of objectivity? Yet once nondualism is accepted as a guiding principle, every aspect of intervention must be rethought.

Overcoming dualism, however, is very difficult. In fact, most theorists have not attempted to make this transition, and many of the ones who have tried have been unsuccessful. For example, evidence of this theoretical shift began to appear in "third force" psychology, symbolic interactionism, and the theories of coping that recognized the ability of cognition to influence behavior. Nonetheless, these views did not extend far enough; in most cases the mind and reality remained juxtaposed. In the following chapters, the attempt will be made to outline in some detail a course that has yet to be fully charted, in terms of specifying the prerequisites of, and the benefits to be derived from, a nondualistic approach to intervention.

Notes

1. U.S. Office of the Federal Register. *United States Statutes at Large*, Vol. 89. (Washington, DC: U.S. Government Printing Office, 1975).

2. Szasz, Thomas. *Insanity*. (New York: John Wiley, 1987), pp. 47–98.

3. Srole, Leo and Anita K. Fisher. "The Midtown Manhattan Longitudinal Study vs. the 'Mental Paradise Lost' Doctrine," *Archives of General Psychiatry* 37, 1980, pp. 209–221; Srole, Leo and Anita K. Fisher. "Debate on Psychiatric Epidemiology," *Archives of General Psychiatry* 37, 1980, pp. 1421–1423.

4. Eysenck, H. J. "A Critique of Contemporary Classification and Diagnosis." In *Contemporary Directions in Psychopathology: Toward the DSM-IV*, ed. Theodore Millon and Gerald Klerman. (New York: Guilford Press, 1986).
5. Wagenfeld, Morton O. and Judith H. Jacobs. "The Community Mental Health Movement: Its Origins and Growth." In *Public Mental Health*, ed. Morton O. Wagenfeld, Paul V. Lemkau, and Blair Justice. (Beverly Hills: Sage, 1982), pp. 46–88.
6. Schutz, Alfred. *The Phenomenology of the Social World*. (Evanston, IL: Northwestern University Press, 1967), pp. 80–81.
7. Ibid., p. 74.
8. Murphy, John W. and John T. Pardeck. "Technologically Mediated Therapy: A Critique," *Social Casework* 67(10), 1986, pp. 605–612.
9. Foucault, Michel. *The Birth of the Clinic*. (New York: Vintage Books, 1975), pp. 34–35.
10. Derrida, Jacques. *Writing and Difference*. (Chicago: University of Chicago Press, 1978), pp. 31–63.
11. Lyotard, Jean-Francois. *The Postmodern Condition: A Report on Knowledge*. (Minneapolis: University of Minnesota Press, 1984), p. 44.
12. Durkheim, Emile. *Pragmatism and Sociology*. (Cambridge: Cambridge University Press, 1963), p. 87.
13. Radden, Jennifer. *Madness and Reason*. (London: George Allen and Harwin, 1985), p. 15.
14. Blumer, Herbert. *Symbolic Interactionism*. (Englewood Cliffs, NJ: Prentice-Hall, 1969), p. 4.
15. Kleinman, Arthur. *Patients and Healers in the Content of Culture*. (Berkeley: University of California Press, 1980), pp. 17–18.
16. Mills, C. Wright. *The Sociological Imagination*. (London: Oxford University Press, 1959), pp. 25–49.
17. Straus, Erwin. *The Primary World of Senses*. (New York: The Free Press, 1963), pp. 3–25.
18. Patton, Michael Quinn. *Utilization-Focussed Evaluation*. (Beverly Hills, CA: Sage, 1978); Patton, Michael Quinn. *Practical Evaluation*. (Beverly Hills, CA: Sage, 1982), pp. 304–305.
19. Stark, Werner. *The Fundamental Forms of Social Thought*. (New York: Fordham University Press, 1963).
20. Naierman, Naomi, Brenda Haskins, Gail Robinson, Christopher Zook, and Douglas Wilson. *Community Mental Health Centers: A Decade Later*. (Cambridge, MA: Abt Books, 1978).
21. Lacan, Jacques. *Ecrits*. (New York: W.W. Norton, 1977), p. 306.
22. Ingleby, David. "Understanding 'Mental Illness'." In *Crucial Psychiatry*, ed. David Ingleby. (New York: Pantheon Books, 1980), pp. 23–71.
23. Lyotard, *The Postmodern Condition*, p. 4.
24. Parsons, Talcott. *The Social System*. (New York: The Free Press, 1951).
25. Ibid., pp. 36–45.
26. Parson, Talcott. *Societies: Evolutionary and Comparative Perspectives*. (Englewood Cliffs, NJ: Prentice-Hall, 1966).
27. Mirowsky, John and Catherine E. Ross. "Psychiatric Diagnosis as Reified Measurement," *Journal of Health and Social Behavior* 30(1), 1989, pp. 11–25.

28. Deleuze, Gilles. "Nomad Thought." In *The New Nietzsche*, ed. David B. Allison. (New York: Delta, 1977), pp. 142–149.

29. Cullen, Francis T. *Rethinking Crime and Deviance Theory.* (Towota, NJ: Rowman and Allanheld, 1984), p. 125.

30. Blumer, *Symbolic Interactionism*, pp. 8–12.

31. Mead, G. H. *Mind, Self and Society.* (Chicago: University of Chicago Press, 1967), p. 46, 67, 78.

32. Derrida, Jacques. *Speech and Phenomena.* (Evanston, IL: Northwestern University Press, 1973), p. 138.

33. Gove, Walter R. "The Labelling Perspective: An Overview." In *The Labelling of Deviance*, ed. Walter R. Gove. (Beverly Hills, CA: Sage, 1980), pp. 9–26.

34. Taylor, Ian, Paul Walton, and Jock Young. *The New Criminology.* (London: Routledge and Kegan Paul, 1973).

35. Lyotard, *The Postmodern Condition.*

36. Kleinman, Arthur. *Rethinking Psychiatry.* (New York: The Free Press, 1988), pp. 1–4.

37. Murphy, John W. and Joseph J. Pilotha. "Research Note: Identifying 'At Risk' Persons in Community Based Research," *Sociology of Health and Illness* 9(1), 1987, pp. 62–75.

38. Bordon, Susan. *The Flight to Objectivity.* (Albany: State University Press of New York, 1987).

39. Holbrook, Terry. "Computer Technology and Behavioral Therapy: A Modern Marriage." In *Technology and Human Service Delivery*, ed. John W. Murphy and John T. Pardeck. (New York: The Haworth Press, 1988), pp. 89–109.

40. Pollner, Melvin. "Sociological and Common-Sense Models of the Labelling Process." In *Ethnomethodology*, ed. Roy Turner. (Middlesex, England: Penguin, 1974), pp. 27–40.

41, Budman, Simon H. and Alan S. Gurman. *Theory and Practice of Brief Therapy.* (New York: The Guilford Press, 1988), pp. 1–25.

42. Marcuse, Herbert. *Eros and Civilization.* (New York: Vintage, 1962), pp. 11–19.

43. Lazarus, Richard S. and Susan Folkman. *Stress, Appraisal, and Coping.* (New York: Springer Publishing Co., 1984).

44. Weingartner, Rudolph H. *Experience and Culture.* (Middletown, CT: Wesleyan University Press, 1962), pp. 16 Ff.

45. Graham, Helen. *The Human Face of Psychology.* (Philadelphia: Open University Press, 1986).

46. Ciompi, Luc. *The Psyche and Schizophrenia.* (Cambridge, MA: Harvard University Press, 1988), pp. 260–261.

47. Murphy, John W. "Cultural Manifestations of Postmodernism," *Philosophy Today* 30(4), 1986, pp. 346–353.

48. Lacan, *Ecrits*, p. 89.

49. Barthes, Roland. *The Rustle of Language.* (New York: Hill and Wang, 1986), p. 160.

50. Miller, J. Hillis. "Stevens' Rock and Criticism as Cure," *Georgia Review* 30(1), 1976, pp. 5–31.

51. Tyler, Stephen A. "Post-Modern Anthropology." In *Discourse and the Social Life of Meaning*, ed. Phyllis Pease Chock and June R. Wyman. (Washington, DC: Smithsonian Institution Press, 1986), pp. 23–49.

52. Barthes, *The Rustle of Language*.
53. Lyotard, Jean-Francois and Jean-Francois Thebaud. *Just Gaming*. (Minneapolis: University of Minnesota Press, 1985).

Chapter Three

The Philosophical and Conceptual Basis of Community-Based Analysis

Intervention as a Science

At the end of the previous chapter the idea is broached that significantly more than technical changes are involved in promoting real community-based intervention. In order to understand the meaning of community-based services, an entirely new perspective on intervention and treatment must be adopted. At this juncture, the term perspective does not simply refer to the logistical strategies used to organize service delivery. For instance, according to the state hospital viewpoint intervention is supposed to be centralized, whereas community-based planning should be decentralized.[1] A maneuver such as this may not result in improved treatment. Stated simply, irrelevant programs of action may still be offered. Only now the physical distance is reduced between providers and clients.

If the benefits of community-based intervention are ever going to be realized, the context of services has to be thoroughly examined. No longer can practitioners assume that illness, diagnosis, and rehabilitation, for example, are value-free concepts.[2] Contrary to the belief that underpinned intervention in the past, becoming increasingly "scientific" may not culminate in the deployment of improved services. In fact, relying on science may have impeded effective service delivery. To understand the thrust of this controversial statement, a break must be made with the traditional views of knowledge, methodology, and social imagery. At the heart of community-based intervention, moreover, should be this conceptual maneuver.

As Michel Foucault rightly notes, intervention has been sustained by Cartesianism.[3] Dualism, as noted in chapter two, has been an integral part of identifying health and illness. Many forms of dualism exist, for example, as is revealed by the distinctions that are made regularly between fact and value, mind and body, and appearance and reality. Especially relevant for this discussion is the separation that is made between subjectivity and objectivity, or what Binswanger calls the "cancer of all psychology up to now."[4] Following this bifurcation, the stage is thought to be set for the development of accurate and thus scientific interventions. Why is this the case?

Objectivity is thought to be sustained by natural laws or other unadulterated means of legitimizing truth.[5] Objectivity, in other words, is not limited like subjectivity. Accordingly, these laws are universal and hold the key to understanding both nature and society. Disciplines such as psychology and sociology, following the lead of medicine and other physical sciences, have remained for the most part dualistic, for the prospect of discovering uniform rules of behavior is still very appealing. In other words, attaining the status of a so-called "hard" science is difficult to resist.

As a result of standardization, the belief is that the damage caused by interpretation can be controlled. This strategy has assumed a couple of forms. First, data have been treated as empirical.[6] By associating knowledge with empirical properties, the role played by interpretation in identifying facts is thought to be diminished. For example, who would claim that physical characteristics are unclear and perhaps unreal? For this reason, a lot of time has been spent attempting to delimit the physiological basis of symptoms. Once this is accomplished sophisticated taxonomies can be formulated, and the "signs" of illness can be classified with little difficulty. This explains why traditionally the focus has been on counting symptoms. Monitoring and enumerating are considered to be activities that do not involve interpretation.

Second, when the collection of these facts is mediated thoroughly by methodology, the influence of interpretation in this process is believed to be decreased.[7] A fully structured psychiatric interview, such as the Diagnostic Interview Schedule, is a good example. Reaching a diagnosis is straightforward because a clinical judgment is produced by following explicit instructions, which supposedly do not need to be deciphered. For adhering to stepwise instructions is an undertaking that is not thought to require any commentary. Accordingly, transforming cognitive into technical operations is believed to neutralize any interpretive task. By employing a "logic tree," which can be easily computerized, a diagnosis can be rendered.[8] Formalizing clinical judgments in this way is certainly expedient, yet can existential considerations really be eliminated? Although standardized operational procedures are supposed to account for "culturally-based" symptoms, neither the protocols nor the raters, in truth, are poised to incorporate this input.

Mediating the research act by methodology inserts a sufficient amount of distance between subjectivity and objectivity. In this way, the illusion can be maintained that data collection and other clinical procedures are unbiased. Judgments are predicated on the facts of a case, rather than assumptions about the identity of knowledge. As a result, "technical competence" becomes a substitute for comprehensive understanding and culturally grounded insights. For the mastery of technique is thought to lead automatically to the collection of high quality data and rational decision making. After all, technical procedures are unaffected by situational exigencies; techniques are implemented in a mechanistic manner. The use of "expert systems," for example, has become quite popular, for their use is thought to improve the reliability of diagnoses.[9]

In some circles, proposals have been made to computerize a wide range of clinical service. With the human element completely eviscerated, the aim of positive science may be finally realized. That is, an objective knowledge base can be generated to guide intervention. But earlier in this chapter the claim was made that such a proposal may be detrimental. This most "recent attack on metaphysics," as Max Horkheimer puts it, may decimate the knowledge acquisition process.[10] How could this be true, considering that objectivity is by definition unbiased? Simply put, by devoting so much attention to objectivity and becoming value-free, many cultural facets of knowledge may be obscured. Because these elements are subjective, they are likely to be either dismissed as unimportant or adjusted to meet certain technical demands. Either way, a significant amount of distortion is interjected into the activity whereby knowledge is procured. How can this manipulation be beneficial? But as long as interpretation is viewed to be an impediment to data collection and decision making, the attempt to move human praxis to the periphery of research or clinical activity will certainly continue.

The argument thus far has been that anti-dualism is the centerpiece of real community-based proposals. Advocates of minority services should avoid the manipulation of knowledge that was just described, for the resulting distortion will not be very productive. Therefore, community-based planning should take place within the social realm that is devastated by dualism. Martin Buber, for example, refers to this as the sphere of the interhuman; the dimension that persons erect and maintain through discourse.[11] Stated differently, intervention should be directed toward the world, which Binswanger defines as "that toward which . . . existence has climbed and according to which it has designed itself."[12] The world should be approached as an existential domain.

Relevant Knowledge

Community-based researchers are not saying that reliable knowledge is unimportant to successful intervention. The questions that are raised pertaining to science and objectivity are not intended to introduce the spectre of nihilism. Instead, the attempt is to promote the awareness that every phase of knowledge acquisition and service planning should reflect *relevant knowledge*. Furthermore, esoteric insight is not a valid substitute for socially confirmed information. Yet, increasingly, funded research and intervention are guided by abstract scientific protocols, obtuse methodologies, and arcane analyses. Mental health professionals have been slow to recognize that no knowledge base is automatically superior to another. But an intervention will be effective only when an appropriate "stock of knowledge" guides this process, no matter how strange this information may at first appear.[13]

In this regard, functionalist, ecological, and medical models of planning and service delivery should be rejected by advocates of community-based intervention. This must be the case, according to Viktor Frankl, because "only an *homme machine* . . . is in need of a *medecin techicien*."[14] According to each of these perspectives, an abstract rendition of social existence is invoked to describe health, illness, and other cultural phenomena. An explanatory "metalanguage"—protocol that are introduced to classify events, but are not subject to serious review—is summoned to reinforce judgments.[15] If the restrictions imposed by subjectivity can be nullified, claim traditionalists, final and complete explanations of behavior may be proposed. Also, unencumbered policy recommendations may finally be forthcoming.

But according to those who actually offer community-based services to minorities, the influence of subjectivity is ubiquitous. Any attempt to purge this factor from consideration is a chimera. The reason for this is quite simple: the human presence is always presupposed in the discovery and utilization of knowledge. Even when the claim is made that particular procedures or taxonomies are value-free, assumptions are advanced about the nature of reality. Furthermore, taking seriously the charge of value freedom may result in bias. Because a set of assumptions is ignored, due to its alleged scientific status, the cultural relevance of those beliefs may not be rigorously scrutinized. Consequently, data are likely to be filtered through assumptions that are socially irrelevant. This sort of science constitutes nothing more than ideology!

Why are assumptions about reality and language no longer easily differentiated? The answer to this query relates to the conception of language extolled by postmodernists. They maintain speech is not a pointer that sometimes reflects accurately reality. Simply put, language does not merely "mirror" or "copy" the physical world.[16] If this were the case, dualism would not be jeopardized. Reality and language would be separate entities that periodically happen to come into contact. Hence truth would be merely temporarily occluded.

Truth, however, is always elusive, because all knowledge must stand in the midst of language. Certainly in the United States, for example, language differences are experienced that relate to ethnicity, geographical region, and social class. As a result, language is laden with definitional and stylistic cultural implications. The hope of attaining *theoria*, or pure vision, is thus shattered.[17] No attempt to transcend language is likely to succeed, for speech mediates every encounter with knowledge. Hence the search for truth should respect the nuances of speech.

As is suggested, all access to truth is indirect. Attempting to bypass the effects of speech through technical rigor is deemed futile. For example, every diagnosis, in line with the etymology of this term, must be understood as an act of knowing that is encumbered by constraints. In this case, these strictures relate to how reality is linguistically deployed by a patient and, on the other hand, approached by a clinician.

Knowledge is the product of a "language game," which can be played in any number of ways. The aim of a community-based researcher, accordingly, should be to enter the game that is underway in a particular locale. Because language use conditions social meaning, speech acts are instrumental to determining the significance of norms, roles and laws. How persons evaluate their behavior, in other words, is vital to classifying properly these actions. "Reality", as Erwin Straus argues, "is not sensed as an impersonal, objective, logical order of events but as the coexistence of the world and myself."[18] Therefore, social sensitivity and competence in the cultural idiom should be operative in both research and treatment.

Community-based practitioners may find the "text" to be an useful metaphor to describe the social world.[19] The point is that order constitutes a script, which must be successfully deciphered. If a book is to be appreciated, the linguistic world expressed by the author must be grasped. Correspondingly, practitioners should be trained to be good readers. To paraphrase Roland Barthes, clinicians and researchers should learn to read in the same manner as citizens write.[20] As a reward for following this axiom, the messages that are buried under layers of social symbolism can be exposed. In this regard, what persons mean when they announce they are ill or well can be understood.

Facts, Truth, and Behavior

Throughout the Western tradition, a penchant has been exhibited for defining truth as *adaequatio rei et intellectus*. Statements are truthful, accordingly, when they reflect adequately reality. Truth, in short, is based on standards that the mind, if trained sufficiently, can mimic. Herein lies the tragedy of the training received by most traditional practitioners in the classroom and the clinic. In short, those who possess significant insight and culturally relevant knowledge have these resources undermined by theories and practices that equate valid knowledge with "objective" techniques. Amedeo Giorgi summarizes this viewpoint with the statement, "*Measurement preceeds existence*."[21] As should be noted, pursuing truth in this way can culminate in deskilling practitioners.

Also pertinent to dualism, opinion must be kept from influencing truth. If opinion should contaminate a diagnosis, for example, the resulting course of action should be considered suspect. In the absence of objectivity, is the only alternative to rely on opinion when making decisions? The answer is no, because neither clinical nor research judgments are speculative, or founded on unsubstantiated claims when a community-based intervention is undertaken. All that is absent are absolute protocols for making decisions. Truth is not outmoded, simply because objective laws are unavailable for review.

The term popularized by Martin Heidegger for defining truth is now relevant. This is *aletheia*.[22] Simply translated, this term means "unconcealedness." Obviously he is making a shift away from the usual "correspondence theory" of truth, whereby an unadulterated referent for knowledge is believed to exist. Instead of reflected, truth must be unconcealed. His point is that truth is not readily visible, but, in the manner suggested by some early Greeks, likes to hide. Where does this hiding occur? Surely truth is not concealed by nature, for physical events are thought to be anchored firmly in time and space. Rather, truth becomes lost in language, once reality cannot be extricated from speech. While making reference to this difficult situation, Jean-Francois Lyotard remarks that truth must "work" if it is to be recognized.[23] A definition of truth may emerge, but only other definitions are available to reinforce this knowledge. Using the textual metaphor, all reading is rereading, for escape from the circle of interpretation is impossible.

Facts may thus be real, but they are not crudely empirical. "Facts are interesting only insofar as we can base our future behavior on them," charges Eugene Minkowski.[24] In other words, knowledge that is not idiosyncratic may be identified, but there are many pitfalls in associating this information with empirical indicators. Most important, subjectivity is simultaneously intersubjectivity. For every language game is public, so to speak, and is accessible to any concerned party. To recognize a fact, therefore, the symbolism that surrounds this knowledge should be explored. Practitioners should learn to probe the nuances of human action, rather than merely classify facts, in order to expose a profound rendition of culture.

Truth does not disappear but subsists within different discursive formations. Foucault, for instance, refers to these contexts as "epistemes," while Erving Goffman calls them "frames."[25] What this accomplishes is to regionalize truth. Within certain constraints, rules can be discerned that serve to differentiate reality from illusion. This maneuver does not relativize truth, because not every rendition of knowledge is acceptable within a given region. Specific assumptions supply the parameters for truth, and these boundaries determine the range of behavior believed to be pathological. Contrary to the proposition made by Durkheim, for example, the identity of the pathological is not universal.[26] Therefore, a researcher or practitioner who is culturally oriented, therefore, is an archaeologist of discursive properties. For concepts such as health and illness are not eternal, but are thoroughly historical and available for serious review and critique.

Investigating Identity and Difference

Obviously deviance relates to normativeness. Indeed, the former presupposes the latter. But norms do not occupy a signorial place, or *topos*, as described by realists once language is understood to mediate reality. Norms do not exist *sui generis*, but are "locally determined."[27] Straus makes this point when he remarks: "As particular beings we live in *perspective*."[28] As opposed to the pure space envisioned by Durkheim, Comte, and Parsons, for example, norms reside in places that are rife with uncertainty. The indeterminacy associated with interpretation is more than an anomaly, because of the pervasiveness of the human presence.

From a community-based perspective, clearing a place where truth can appear should not be the aim of methodology. In addition to being futile, this practice ignores the linguistic foundation of facts. Methodologists, therefore, should not concentrate on logistical rigor, but on becoming "culturally competent."[29] Why are clearings that are generated experimentally impossible to create? Answer: Contrived facts that have been stripped of personal expression always remain linguistic artifacts. Hence becoming conversant with various language games should be of prime importance, rather than creating unnatural domains where facts can appear.

At first this methodological shift may sound bizarre, for technical acuity and the resulting value-freedom are viewed typically as leading to truth. But if truth is embedded in discursive practices, perhaps intervention should be value-based? Maybe the recognition of values would be a more effective principle to underpin research and clinical practice? Enticing values into the open may be more appropriate than obscuring them through the use of elaborate techniques.

Instead of concealing values, a community-based methodology should be viewed as an invitation to dialogue. As opposed to harvesting facts, becoming engaged with meaning should be the thrust of any inquiry. Facts should be approached as a fickle lover, who cannot be taken for granted. Discovering the mood of this person is vital to productive interaction, and, in this context, requires that a series of subcultural tests be met. Likewise, cajoling persons into revealing something about themselves demands that intimate contact with them be established. Otherwise, practitioners are only skating on the surface of meaning, unable to penetrate the arena of primordial commitments and beliefs. How can this kind of superficial investigation be fruitful?

To provide an example, Canquilhem states that diseases are "polysemic," or speak in numerous ways.[30] In order to comprehend these problems practitioners must learn to speak correctly rather than simply identify and manage cases. Does this mean that gathering information inevitably must become haphazard or sloppy? Absolutely not. Nonetheless, what practitioners are doing when they gather information must assume a new form.

In fact, practitioners may have to become more rigorous than in the past. Methodology, simply defined, relates to ways of gathering information; systematic procedures to attain an end.[31] Formerly, rigor was equated with becoming internally consistent. If reliability could be guaranteed, the procedural flaws indicative of error could be minimized. By following certain methodological rules, errors could be randomized. Insuring internal consistency, however, is relatively easy. All that is required is technical skill. Mastering certain techniques is not a very complicated undertaking, compared to what should be done when undertaking a community-based intervention.

Now interactional or communicative competence should be the focus of attention. Simply stated, this means that all data collection strategies should be designed to accommodate the "pragmatic thrust" of language, thereby facilitating a proper understanding of the social world.[32] This has important implications. Definitions of reality, rather than preordained empirical indices, should inform the design of data collection instruments. Data collection categories, in short, should be developed from culturally relevant cognitive operations. In this way, dialogue with citizens is possible.

But if all knowledge is mediated by interpretation, methodologies are also not value-free. In order to engage clients or citizens in discourse, therefore, the linguistic categories that sustain a method must be brought to a level of conscious awareness. As long as the claim of value-freedom is retained, this reflexive posture will not be seen as necessary.[33] Nonetheless, once the cognitive basis of methodology is recognized, the rationale for merging this domain with the linguistic scheme that persons adopt to circumscribe reality should become clear. Doubtless, this *modus operandi* is very difficult. First criticisms about value-freedom must be broached and understood, while, second, building methodologies that are linguistically pertinent must be inaugurated.

Because methodologies cannot be viewed as related passively to reality, their linguistic relevance becomes of paramount importance. Both persons and methodologies engage and thus shape the world, thereby implying that their respective linguistic presuppositions must be merged if undistorted knowledge is to be acquired. Hans-Georg Gadamer, for instance, refers to this process as "fusing" horizons of expectations.[34]

In a manner of speaking, methodologies and persons have expectations about the world. Persons deploy reality linguistically, while clients and facts are classified by methodologies on the basis of theoretical constructs. Hence communication is possible only when these expectations are aligned. Stated differently, understanding results from persons "reading" the world in a similar manner.[35] "Double-rapport" is the key to successful community-based intervention, rather than logistical refinement and value-freedom.[36] Practitioners and citizens must confirm one another, or dialogue will not occur.

Does this change in thinking require that every traditional methodological technique must be abandoned? All that is necessary, instead, is that methodological categories used to classify material reflect the linguistic modalities persons employ to shape reality. In anthropological parlance, developing "emic" approaches to gathering information should be given a high priority. For unless the ways in which persons make sense out of reality is given consideration, the chances are increased that their conceptions of health and illness will be misconstrued. Any serious investigation, therefore, should incorporate the element of ethnography.

Although this need for ethnographic skills will be discussed in greater detail in chapter five, a few points should be made at this juncture. First, similar empirical indices do not necessarily have the same meaning. Second, contextual sensitivity is not acquired at the expense of truth. And third, recognizing that generalizations are limited is not necessarily the sign of an immature science.

Some critics charge, however, that this approach to gathering information precludes the possibility of making comparisons. Nothing but idiosyncratic data are available. Many practitioners will recall that the same argument was adopted to discourage the use of "Goal Attainment Scaling."[37] This method of treatment planning was invented to permit the formation of culturally relevant treatment goals. Yet allowing clients to propose very personal objectives does not necessarily prevent general statements from being made about the overall success of an intervention.

What is wrong with specifying the number of persons who have achieved their individual goals? Only when dualism is accepted does everyone have to achieve a similar goal. At this juncture is where the need to rethink standard intervention protocol becomes readily apparent. If clients and communities are to be influenced by intervention, the realization should be promoted that a uniform base for comparisons is not always appropriate. More relevant may be very specific statements about goal achievement, comparisons between persons who have a similar problem *and* cultural context, or extremely qualified claims about the factors that lead to successful treatment. Practitioners should remember that the idiosyncratic nature of communities often prevents the indefinite extension of generalizations! This is not necessarily a methodological problem, but one that is related to the study of humans.

In terms of a community-based assessment, the mechanism adopted for making comparisons should not be viewed as a scheme that is impervious to interpretation. Further, the human ability to assimilate differences and make distinctions should be operative. Thus differences may be comparable if they are "thematic," or understood to be relevant to one another. Relevance, in turn, is based on meaning, rather than empirical indices. Because different empirical indices may have identical meanings, these differences can be merged. In short, ostensibly different base-lines may be similar and readily compared.

Order and the Focus of Intervention

Throughout the history of the Western intellectual tradition, an Archimedean point has been sought to substantiate order. The belief has been that order cannot be based on something as capricious as subjectivity. Therefore, a reality *sui generis* must be available to sanction behavior. Order, as described by Marcuse, must be "affirmative."[38] Hence no mistakes can be made about normative expectations, because the dimensions of reality are abundantly clear. As is suggested, most attempts to conceptualize order have had a definite realistic cast.

Various structural metaphors have been employed to create the image that order is autonomous. At various times the social world has been described to consist of "roles," "networks," and "subsystems." In each case, the point has been to suggest that social reality is substantial, or a force that can constrain persons. Roles are reciprocally related, for example, and thus interaction is guaranteed. Hence, clearly delineated operations specify how interaction should proceed.

The focus of intervention, accordingly, has been these obtrusive structures. Examining role conflicts and adjusting persons to societal demands, for instance, are the tasks undertaken traditionally by practitioners.[39] Externalizing the thrust of intervention, both in terms of research and therapy, has resulted in practitioners being concerned with normalcy, instead of health and illness. How closely a person conforms to the norm appears to be the test of successful intervention. However, health has only a precarious relationship to normalcy.

To understand the meaning of health from a community-based perspective, new social imagery has to be invented. Conceptualizing the social world strictly in structural terms is now passé, for suggested by this gambit is that the basis of order is unaffected by subjectivity. Order, like all types of knowledge, represents a discursive formation. In other words, a linguistic bond is sufficient to hold society together. As a result, health should be considered to represent a linguistic category, rather than a structural imperative. Normalcy, in point of fact, is associated with role demands, while health is a human construct.

What reality represents, in terms of a social system, is a patchwork of different linguistic domains.[40] In each one, a slightly different linguistic game may be in operation. This is not to say that certain games are always prevented from dominating others, but that social existence is not fundamentally monolithic. A practitioner, who adopts a multi-cultural perspective, moreover, should try to insure that the integrity of each game is preserved, or health may not be promoted by intervention.[41] Consistent with a community-based orientation, Frankl states that real healing can occur only if behavioral change takes place within a client's "world view."[42]

For quite some time a debate has raged over the nature of a community.[43] As with order in general, the tendency has been to describe a community in structural terms. Physical markers, such as ethnic traits, institutions, and geography, have been used to identify these locations. While these obtrusive features may have some validity, they obtain their significance from the way reality is conceptualized.[44] A community, in short, constitutes a "domain of commitment"—an intersection of language games—where definitions of reality begin to overlap and common knowledge bases emerge. "Attuned space" is the phrase used by Binswanger to describe the place where a community exists.[45] These locations do not extend indefinitely, but have boundaries that relate to reality assumptions. "Multiple realities" exist, claims Alfred Schutz, and the tasks of a culturally sensitive community-based practitioner should be to discover where one begins and another ends.[46] Accordingly, he notes that the worlds of health and madness are "infinitely numerous." Normalcy is thus impossible to identify with absolute certainty.

Because these realities reflect differences in knowledge bases, "epistemological participation" should be the hallmark of culturally relevant intervention. This means that practitioners should become cognizant of the various modalities of experience that constitute reality. This process has nothing to do with whether or not those who are studied or treated are liked or valued, or the reality in question is considered to be ultimately normal. Instead, epistemological participation relates to apprehending the discursive practices that unite persons into a community.

Due to the existential nature of a community, extreme care should be taken when attempting to generalize about norms. Hence only "middle range" analytical models should be acceptable. In other words, theories that are neither idiosyncratic nor abstract should be formulated. Considering the linguistic nature of reality, Donald Davidson states that "passing theory" most adequately describes the nature of human existence.[47] Because a provisional set of interpretations is the only safeguard against chaos, theory building should take place within this linguistic realm that unites persons. A community-based model of health and illness, therefore, should be sensitive to the surprises that can occur when players of different language games come into contact. In this regard, as Davidson notes, misinterpretations should not be dismissed as mistakes, if the aim is to foster mutual understanding between practitioners and clients.

If the purpose of intervention is to reflect reality, practitioners should not be disappointed that social existence is epistemologically pluralistic. And why should "grounded theory" be eschewed?[48] If reality is a patchwork, should the development of formalized models be the aim of practitioners? Of course not. Surely situationally relevant interventions are worthwhile discoveries, and efficacious explanations are valuable. Simply because knowledge is localized, does not mean it should be devalued.

Reflexivity and Intervention

Building reflexivity into research and treatment should be very important to a community-based practitioner. In the early 1970s Alvin Gouldner paid some attention to this issue, while currently a key exponent of reflexivity is Niklas Luhmann.[49] Although neither of these authors addresses the relationship between intervention and reflexivity, their message is clear. That is, unreflective methodologies are crude and unresponsive to social demands. Their recommendation, accordingly, is that social scientists should build this mechanism into research and other aspects of intervention.

What is reflexivity? Simply defined, reflexivity is a process whereby the validity of techniques or other phenomena is temporarily placed in abeyance. Self-criticism is key to this activity. Therefore, rather than accepted in a straightforward manner, the validity of a research or clinical practice is reconstructed during each application. As a result, the likelihood that the reality of an event will be naively approached is reduced. When the social context and other sources of assumptions that are instrumental to determining validity are called into question, the appropriateness of an intervention is not left to chance.

Obviously reflexivity is not a part of most interventions. Actually, a conscious effort is made regularly to exclude reflexivity from the training of practitioners. To interject reflexivity into a research methodology is considered to be a formula for failure. After all, reflexivity is anathema to value-freedom. Jacques Ellul goes so far as to suggest that reflexivity unsettles techniques, and thus threatens the acquisition of technical acuity.[50] Why would a rational practitioner want to court disaster in this way?

Nonetheless, according to advocates of community-based intervention, the claim that facts, methodologies, and social reality are imbued with values is hard to deny. Therefore, why should the charade be maintained that judgments do not infest interventions? What reflexivity does is to bring these cognitive acts out into the open, so their relevance can be debated. If objectivity is undermined at any time during an intervention, this occurs when research strategies and clinical instruments are formulated. But because of their linguistic character, methodological techniques or psychological tests can never be objective in the Cartesian sense. As a result of reflection, the point is made clear that interventions exist in situ and are replete with values.

Yet usefulness is not destroyed by a lack of objectivity! For example, can a clinical test be useful, without being objective? The answer given by a community-based practitioner should be yes. In this context, data are useful when they represent the reality that is present within a particular experiential domain. "Interpretive adequacy," writes Weber, is essential to gathering this sort of data, rather than objectivity.[51] Clearly having data that allow behavior to be predicted is worthwhile, yet obtaining this knowledge is unrelated to Cartesianism. Reflexivity, moreover, helps to outline the parameters of utility, as a result of exposing both methodological and reality assumptions.

Following the institution of reflexivity, several important points are illustrated. First, perception is simultaneously interpretation. Barthes makes this point when he says there is no such thing as an innocent reading of the world.[52] Second, assumptions about reality are invented, rather than discovered. Certain presuppositions, therefore, are not automatically more rational than others. For example, rationality in one language game may represent irrationality in another. Third, generalizations can be extended only as far as social experiences will allow. Hence, locally appropriate statements should be of interest to a community-based practitioner. In this context, methodological and conceptual adequacy are social rather than technical issues.

Earlier the statement was made that community-based practitioners should be concerned with health, as opposed to normalcy. In view of the images of knowledge and order that have been advanced, distinguishing these two factors should not be considered odd. Health is a personal and sometimes a collective determination, based on principles that are localized, whereas in the behavioral sciences normalcy usually relates to uniform standards. No wonder Binswanger remarks that a concern for normalcy may prevent someone from becoming a good practitioner.[53] Emphasizing normalcy, in other words, may block access to a client's or community's knowledge base, and thus inaccurate and ineffective interventions are likely to be prescribed. Community-based practitioners should not be blinded by normalcy, thereby stripping intervention of ideology.

The point is that without reflexivity, intervention is often ideological. Conceptual schemes that are identified as scientific are seldom criticized, and thus the social basis of norms tends to be obscured. When this is the case, abstract patients are treated, while deviance and successful treatment are measured against standard that are not socially corroborated.[54] To a practitioner who is culturally sensitive, ideology such as this is debilitating and, in the long run, disruptive. When clients believe the delivery of services should be culturally sensitive, resentment, indifference, and withdrawal are likely to occur when this expectation is unmet. Now, in addition to providing irrelevant services, the ire of a community may be raised. Once this vicious cycle is instigated, how can effective treatment ever be provided?

But through the use of culturally adroit interventions, the production of ideology is avoided. And once this happens, and a community's trust is gained, intervention strategies will surely improve. As a result of recognizing that science can become an ideology, political and social critiques become a part of intervention. The means is thus available to prevent social services from becoming a vehicle for social control. Instead of abstract ideas, a client's well-being, no matter where treatment leads, guides intervention. In this sense, a community-based intervention can bring to fruition the aims of therapy (*therapeia*). Consistent with what the early Greeks had in mind, intervention that is community-based restores a community to its own sense of well-being, regardless of how this condition may be defined by social gatekeepers.[55] Community-based intervention should not simply occur in the community, but, more important, should foster the *ethos* of clients.

Notes

1. Turkle, Sherry. "French Anti-psychiatry." In *Critical Psychiatry*, ed. David Ingleby. (New York: Pantheon, 1980), pp. 150–183.
2. Murphy, John W., and Joseph J. Pilotta. "Community-Based Evaluation for Criminal Justice Planning," *Social Service Review* 57(3), 1983, pp. 465–476.
3. Foucault, Michel. *Madness and Civilization*. (New York: Random House, 1973).
4. May, Rollo, Ernest Angel, and Henri F. Ellenberger, (eds.). *Existence: A New Dimension in Psychiatry and Psychology*. (New York: Basic Books, 1959), p. 11.
5. Guattari, Felix. *Molecular Revolution*. (New York: Penguin, 1984), pp. 82–107.
6. Marcuse, Herbert. *One-Dimensional Man*. (Boston: Beacon Press, 1964), pp. 56–83.
7. Ibid., pp. 170–199.
8. Murphy, John W., and John T. Pardeck. "Dehumanization, Computers, and Clinical Practice," *Journal of Social Behavior and Personality* 3(1), 1988, pp. 107–116.
9. Murphy, John W. and John T. Pardeck. "Non-technical Correctives for High-tech Systems in Social Service Agencies," *The Clinical Supervisor* 6(2), 1988, pp. 63–73.

10. Horkheimer, Max. *Critical Theory*. (New York: Seabury Press, 1972), pp. 132–187.

11. Buber, Martin. *I and Thou*. (New York: Charles Scribner's Sons, 1970).

12. Binswanger, Ludwig. "The Existential Analysis School of Thought." In *Existence: A New Dimension in Psychiatry and Psychology*, ed. Rollo May, Ernest Angel and Henri F. Ellenberger. (New York: Basic Books, 1959), pp. 191–213.

13. Berger, Peter L. and Thomas Luckmann. *The Social Construction of Reality*. (Garden City, NY: Doubleday, 1967), pp. 41–46.

14. Frankl, Viktor. *The Unconscious God*. (New York: Simon and Schuster, 1975), p. 20.

15. Lyotard, *The Postmodern Condition: A Report on Knowledge*. (Minneapolis: University of Minnesota Press, 1984), xxiii.

16. Rorty, Richard. *Philosophy and the Mirror of Nature*. (Princeton: Princeton University Press, 1979).

17. de Man, Paul. *The Resistance to Theory*. (Minneapolis: University of Minnesota Press, 1986), pp. 3–20.

18. Straus, Erwin W. *Phenomenological Psychology*. (New York: Garland Publishing, 1980), p. 294.

19. Brown, Richard Harvey. *Society as Text*. (Chicago: University of Chicago Press, 1987).

20. Barthes, Roland. *Criticism and Truth*. (Minneapolis: University of Minnesota Press, 1987), p. 84.

21. Giorgi, Amedeo. *Psychology as a Human Science*. (New York: Harper and Row, 1970), p. 65.

22. Heidegger, Martin. *Being and Time*. (New York: Harper and Brothers, 1962), pp. 262 ff.

23. Lyotard, Jean-Francois. *Driftworks*. (New York: Semiotextle, 1984), p. 35.

24. Minkowski, Eugene. *Lived Time*. (Evanston, IL: Northwestern University Press, 1979), p. 185.

25. Foucault, Michel. *The Archaeology of Knowledge*. (New York: Harper and Row, 1972). Goffman, Erving. *Frame Analysis*. (New York: Harper and Row, 1974).

26. Durkheim, Emile. *The Rules of Sociological Method*. (New York: Free Press, 1964).

27. Lyotard, *The Postmodern Condition*, p. 61.

28. Straus, *Phenomenological Psychology*, p. 322.

29. Habermas, Jurgen. "Toward a Theory of Communicative Competence." In *Recent Sociology*, no. 2, ed. Hans Petel Dreitzel. (New York: Macmillan, 1970), pp. 115–148.

30. Canquilhem, Georges. *On the Normal and the Pathological*. (Dordrecht, Netherlands: D. Reidel, 1978), pp. 105–118.

31. Van Kaam, Adrian. *Existential Foundations of Psychology*. (Pittsburgh, PA: Duquesne University Press, 1966), pp. 256–257.

32. Habermas, "Toward A Theory of Communicative Competence."

33. Murphy and Pilotta, "Community-Based Evaluation for Criminal Justice Planning."

34. Gadamer, Hans-Georg. *Truth and Method*. (New York: Crossroad, 1982), pp. 269ff.

35. Barthes, Roland. *The Rustle of Language*. (New York: Hill and Wang, 1986), p. 54.

36. Murphy, John W. "Deconstruction, Discourse, and Liberation," *Social Science Information* 26(2), 1987, pp. 417–433.
37. Kiresuk, Thomas J. and Robert E. Sherman. "Goal Attainment Scaling: A General Method for Evaluating Comprehensive Community Mental Health Programs," *Community Mental Health Journal* 4(6), 1968, pp. 443–453.
38. Marcuse, Herbert. *Negations.* (Boston: Beacon Press, 1969), pp. 88–133.
39. Deleuze, Gilles and Félix Guattari. *Anti-Oedipus.* (New York: The Viking Press, 1977).
40. Perelman, Chaim. *The New Rhetoric and the Humanities.* (Dordrecht, Netherlands: D. Reidel, 1979), pp. 58–60.
41. Lyotard, Jean-Francois and Jean-Loup Thébaud. *Just Gaming.* (Minneapolis: University of Minnesota Press, 1985), pp. 99–100.
42. Frankl, Viktor E. *The Doctor and the Soul.* (New York: Alfred A. Knopf, 1963), pp. 15-20.
43. Heller, Kenneth. "The Return to Community," *American Journal of Psychology* 17(1), 1989, pp. 1–15.
44. Perelman, *The New Rhetoric and the Humanities*, pp. 159–163.
45. Ellenberger, Henri F. "A Clinical Introduction to Psychiatric Phenomenology and Existential Analysis." In *Existence*, ed. May, Angel, and Ellenberger, pp. 92–124.
46. Schutz, Alfred. *Collected Papers*, Vol. I. (The Hague: Nijhoff, 1962), pp. 207–259.
47. Rorty, Richard, *Contingency, Irony, and Solidarity.* (Cambridge: Cambridge University Press, 1989), pp. 14 ff.
48. Glaser, Barney G. and Anselm L. Strauss. *The Discovery of Grounded Theory.* (Chicago: Aldine, 1967).
49. Gouldner, Alvin. *The Coming Crisis in Western Sociology.* (New York: Basic Books, 1920), pp. 481–512. Luhmann, Niklas, *The Differentiation of Society.* (New York: Columbia University Press, 1982), pp. 324–362.
50. Ellul, Jacques. *The Technological Society.* (New York: Random House, 1964).
51. Weber, Max. *Economy and Society*, Vol. I. (Berkeley: University of California Press, 1978), pp. 8–15.
52. Barthes, Roland. *Writing Degree Zero.* (New York: Hill and Wang, 1968), p. 16.
53. Binswanger, Ludwig. *Being-in-the-World.* (London: Basic Books, 1963), pp. 206–221.
54. Foucault, *The Birth of the Clinic.* (New York: Pantheon, 1973), pp. 3–21.
55. Cushman, Robert E. *Therapeia.* (Chapel Hill: University of North Carolina Press, 1958).

Chapter Four

Medicalization and the Degradation of Culture

Culture in Medicine

A truly revolutionary period of experimentation with community-based intervention is underway in general medicine. Significant studies have been funded to determine how best to approach communities and specific cultural groups with various types of health interventions. For example, persons are learning how to detect breast anomalies, lower the risk of coronary heart disease, quit smoking, and monitor diabetes. Programs such as these are formulated currently as field trials that utilize multiple methods of community entry. Their common goal is to determine the types of approaches that produce desired health behaviors in specific communities and among linguistically diverse ethnic groups. Although there remains some skepticism regarding their efficacy within the medical community, there is a general appreciation that this type of experimentation will require time, resources, and cultural sensitivity to succeed. Moreover, there is a widespread belief that the results will justify the effort.

In contrast to this experience, neither the will nor the technology has been forthcoming in psychiatry to launch community-based experiments similar to those seen in general medicine. Why? The reasons are far-reaching, and extend to the core of the dilemma faced by the mental health field as a science and public health discipline. This chapter will assess critically the array of issues responsible for the general retreat of psychiatry from community intervention.

Psychiatry in Medicine

Customarily, psychiatry has been relegated to the periphery of medical science. This sad fact has had serious implications for the growth of the field. Specifically, public mental health receives marginal support for research and services, and this has meant fewer opportunities for high status careers in this discipline. Psychiatry, in short, has not been perceived as an essential branch of medicine. There are several reasons for this.

The perplexing nature of behavioral and mood disorders, combined with the culture-specific context required for interpreting mental illness, make imposing the same standards found in general medicine for establishing etiology and classifying disorders very difficult in psychiatry. The cross-cultural literature on depression, for example, documents the diverse ways that depression can be revealed. Depression can be purely somatic, while at other times anger is the primary feature of this problem.[1] To further illustrate this point, among non-Hispanic whites in the United States demoralization and hopelessness are chiefly linked to depression.[2]

The interrelationship of social and biological factors has limited the development of verifiable explanatory models with regard to analyzing mental illness. In turn, this has brought into question the integrity of psychiatry as a medical specialty. There is nothing as neat as germ theory in psychiatry, with a demonstrated ability for depicting pathology, so that hard "markers" of risk can be discovered. As Klerman notes: "In general medicine, the descriptions of symptoms (syndromes) are usually validated by being correlated with anatomic pathology or with histochemical changes."[3] Klerman goes on to say that the equivalent in contemporary psychiatry is the use of magnetic resonance imaging and positron emission tomography to confirm brain anomalies.

However, these approaches assume that mental illness has a universal biological basis, and fail to heed the obvious evidence that psychiatry must deal with values, norms, beliefs, imagery, ideation, and social history. Mirowsky and Ross have noted that there is a big difference, and potentially a misleading one, between the way people really see their personal distress and how a disorder is simulated by DSM-III protocol. Indeed, these writers conclude that the benefits, either scientific or therapeutic, associated with the current diagnostic paradigm are not obvious.

> The absence of gold standards, the paucity and the uncertain relevance of latent biological classes, and the symptom factors that bear little resemblance to diagnostic 'syndromes' lead us to believe that psychiatric diagnoses, whether simulated or clinical, are mythical

entities. The diagnoses add nothing to the direct assessment of the feelings, thoughts, acts, and histories (or biochemistries) on which they are based. On the contrary, they degrade information, obscure patterns, and misdirect attention.[4]

Therefore, the diagnostic models appropriate to somatic medicine and public health are difficult to transpose into the mental health context. In addition, the parameters and endpoints of many psychiatric disorders are indeterminate because mental illness has many idioms of expression.[5] Hence, the course and onset of a disorder are often unpredictable, even when biological precursors may be strongly implicated, such as in the case of schizophrenia or manic-depressive bipolar illness. This inability to exert rigor over etiologic and taxonomic issues has proven to be problematic and gradually lowered the position of psychiatry in the medical pantheon. Proponents of the "medicalization" perspective, such as Klerman, admit that the case for diagnostic validity is weak; however, making a diagnosis is not viewed to be simply an act of reification. Rather, diagnosis is the cornerstone of medical science, and recent advances in biological psychiatry and psychopharmacology confirm the scientific importance of this process.[6]

Nonetheless, advocates of medicalization fail to appreciate two important points. First, political and economic factors, not just scientific ones, explain the preoccupation psychiatry has had with diagnostic classification. Second, the use of DSM-III (or DSM-III-R) criteria for achieving reliable diagnosis, assuming this could ever be achieved, has little relevance for planning or delivering community mental health services to cultural minorities. There is no reason to believe that interventions based on medical taxonomies will be more efficacious in lowering mental illness morbidity rates than social interventions. In fact, the historical parallel in nineteenth-century Europe drawn from general medicine appears to demonstrate the opposite result. Mortality declined more as a consequence of changes in social conditions, such as improved literacy and better housing, than as a result of more refined medical classification and intervention.[7]

Rather than accepting at face value that mental illness is qualitatively distinct from somatic medicine, but no less important, the attempt has been made by the psychiatric establishment to emulate aspects of clinical medicine in a quest for respectability. This is not stated with the motive of maligning biological research. Certainly, biomedical research related to the etiology of brain dysfunctions should continue to be supported. Yet discrediting sociocultural studies or denying that many types of mental illness may have a social remedy is inappropriate in order to justify biomedical research. However, the key shortcoming of psychiatric research is that the aim is to isolate discrete empirical criteria for identifying disorders, based on the dubious assumption that these maladies are distributed universally and have a single meaning.[8] Furthermore, specific medication-based therapies for discrete disorders are thought to provide a reliable mode of mental health intervention.[9]

This "push" to become a hard science has done a great disservice to community mental health, as a result of creating the illusion that mental illness is like any somatic illness and has a uniform onset and course, along with categorical impairments. As with somatic illnesses, intervention is thought to be improved when the biological mechanisms that are involved are thoroughly understood. Therefore, accepting this model means that "community mental health" does not exist, since the locus of the problem is assumed to be the individual, and this is where interventions are mostly targeted. This emphasis reduces the relevance of social factors, because a biological etiology is presupposed.

This fascination with taxonomy and biomedical research is maintained even though practitioners and researchers generally agree that most individuals who need mental health services are usually experiencing acute psychophysiological discomfort or personal disorganization, rather than chronic mental disorders.[10] As such, they are usually the victims of social processes and circumstances. Also, ignored by the medical model are the implications for day-to-day operations of CMHCs. For example, the typical depression patient is dealt with in much the same way as one who is schizophrenic because of the tendency to extend models of chronic illness to acute patients. This is not only a disservice to a large class of patients, but also a faulty model is provided for training clinical staff about stress reactions and the environmental issues related to differences in lifestyles.

Even in instances of specific disorders where a biologic etiology is strongly suggested, cultural definitions cannot be ignored. After all, deviance is a social determination. Cultural definitions are important in determining whether a behavior is treated, formally or informally, in addition to the type of treatment that is believed to be appropriate.[11] Therefore, the preoccupation with whether a disorder is real or imaginary has little correspondence with personal experience. Nor are official diagnoses linked to the process whereby members of cultural groups recognize, respond to, or assist others who are having psychological problems. In short, personal experiences exist no matter how they are viewed by clinical experts.

The biomedical approach simply ignores cultural information, thereby obfuscating the social context of mental illness. For example, even if rigorous classification is attainable, the objective of improved mental health services for minorities will not necessarily be achieved. In fact, most of the persons who meet criteria for a DSM-III psychiatric disorder will never be treated by mental health professionals. These individuals may never realize that they are suffering from a psychiatric disorder. Moreover, many minority group members, especially immigrants, are even less likely to perceive themselves as having a mental health problem.

This point is supported by findings from recent epidemiologic field surveys, especially the multisite Epidemiologic Catchment Area project (ECA). Without benefit of community survey data, Regier et al. estimated that one person in five with a diagnosable psychiatric disorder is treated by a mental health professional, while a similar proportion is seen by a physician.[12] But the ECA data indicate quite a different profile. For example, the observed utilization of medical and mental health providers for psychiatric problems is only half of what Regier predicted, in other words, twenty percent overall. Furthermore, data for Mexican Americans at the Los Angeles site are even more compelling. As a group, only eleven percent of Mexican Americans who were diagnosed as potential "cases" ever used physicians or mental health providers to resolve a psychiatric problem.[13] Among minimally acculturated Mexican Americans, only four percent were treated by mental health specialists, and an additional two percent went to a physician for services. Suggested by these data is that "official" DSM-III diagnostic ratings and informal evaluations of personal functioning are in serious disagreement. The obvious discrepancy between utilization rates of Mexican Americans and respondents at other ECA sites underscores the importance of the cultural component in recognizing and responding to psychiatric disorders.

The "medicalization" of mental health has set back minority mental health research, training, and services. According to the biomedical paradigm, cultural differences are not at the core of the issues related to etiology. However, despite this scientific posturing, there is little evidence that the acceptability of psychiatry in general medicine has increased. Indeed, schools of public health have only recently begun to accept the study of mental illness as a legitimate specialization, and little attention is paid in medical schools to psychiatry in training students or residents.[14] The result of this situation is that physicians have little knowledge about mental health problems, and thus they commonly adopt an attitude that mental health is irrelevant to general medicine. Paradoxically, many patients, perhaps even a majority, have primary psychiatric problems that are masked by health complaints.[15] Many other patients have secondary psychological problems that are provoked by their somatic conditions. Nonetheless, most people who seek treatment and also have serious psychiatric problems are treated by medical personnel, while the true nature of the "problem" experienced by many clients is never understood or treated because of the insensitivity of physicians.

In addition to the historical marginality of psychiatry in medicine, the decline of the community mental health orientation has been accelerated by interest in biological psychiatry. In a sense, this can be seen as part of the "back to basics" movement, where many social activities related to intervention are eliminated because resources are concentrated on managing the chronic mental disease, for example, of seriously disordered psychotic patients. This shift is, in part, a consequence of deinstitionalization, but also is consistent with the biomedical model. In short, this type of patient appears to be less amenable to traditional social interventions, and is more likely to be rendered manageable by the use of medication. Furthermore, services are being realigned in a familiar medical care configuration, thus homogenizing the patient population and removing services from minority communities, except for those treatment and residential settings that are intended for use by clients who are seriously ill.

Mental Health, Power, Politics, and Policy

These trends are likely to have implications for training mental health professionals, the growth of the knowledge base, and the organization and delivery of mental health services. From the standpoint of achieving a more desirable state of preparedness, and serving culturally diverse populations, none of these trends can be considered favorable.

There are likely to be serious repercussions in the formal training of mental health and allied practitioners. As noted, physicians receive minimal exposure to mental health information, cross-cultural training, or prevention in medical school, and thus are not rewarded for acquiring this type of information. Hence, the health beliefs and personal practices of minorities are especially neglected. In their clinical work, M.D.s simply avoid dealing with the psychological or emotional aspects of cases, because they are exposed mostly to genetic and biochemical models of mental illness. Also, future clinical psychologists will likely be trained in biomedical models of mental illness. Despite abundant developments in the subfields of behavioral medicine and health psychology, social issues related to mental health have rarely been incorporated into intervention models. Moreover, psychologists are seldom trained in transcultural research or intervention. And many social workers simply avoid addressing public mental health issues and plan to fill institutional positions or operate private practices. The end result of these trends, if sustained, will be to deplete the number of community mental health professionals who have any knowledge about how cultural differences affect intervention.

This emphasis on biomedical research will create an asymmetry in the knowledge base. Shortchanged will be social psychiatry, social epidemiology, community psychology, sociocultural research, and community intervention studies. This is especially exasperating, because the opportunity now exists for linking these various types of research. For example, epidemiological research can be combined with sociocultural observation, in order to encourage a socially correct interpretation of empirical indicators. Many of the conceptual problems discussed in chapters two and three, especially related to the limitations imposed by dualism, could be addressed by a synthesis of epidemiological and ethnomethodological research. Regrettably, this merger will not likely occur, because of the disproportionate investment of resources in biomedical research, and the unfavorable attitude toward social science research, especially ethnographic studies, that now inundates the major funding agencies.

One direct result is that minority researchers are discouraged by the lack of support and the endless maze of political-bureaucratic machinations at the federal level, as is currently the case at the National Institute of Mental Health. Unfortunately, few alternatives exist for underwriting mental health research and intervention trials. State departments of mental health are not equipped or disposed to either undertake or fund this type of research. Additionally, private foundations are mostly interested in developing services networks for the chronically mentally ill.

The scenario, as depicted above, has made the issue of community-based intervention for cultural minorities, in addition to ethnographic research, appear to be a cry in the dark. Nobody is listening. The policies and resources of state and federal agencies are oriented toward fulfilling a different policy agenda. Attempts have been made by some prominent politicians to confront agency directors about the policy of abandoning minority mental health, but there has been only symbolic responses to this prodding. All in all, many psychiatrists appear to be satisfied that research is back where it belongs in the clinic or lab, rather than in the community where so much uncertainty is possible. Furthermore, the federal government has divorced itself from the providers of community mental health services, subsequent to the inception of the Block Grant program. Fundamentally, this situation is a political one, and change can only come about through this avenue. Until a new direction is established at the highest levels of government, current trends are likely to continue unabated.

Social and Organizational Factors Affecting Intervention

Considering the shortcomings of the community mental health experience, various inadequacies need to be corrected in order to improve services to minorities. Serious study should be directed to (1) the social context of illness and (2) organization factors that impede service delivery. Indeed, these areas are symbiotic, because they both affect the willingness of individuals to recognize that they have a mental health problem, seek information about possible treatment alternatives, select and utilize specific services providers or interventions, and complete treatment.

The Social Basis of Mental Illness

The recognition of mental illness is not automatic, nor is there uniformity in the remedy for its abatement. For the most part, mental health practitioners have ignored this fact, and instead have adopted a service model centered around "demanders": that is, those who find their way to providers and elect to continue treatment are served. Obviously, this approach abrogates the basic premise of true community involvement and is more akin to opening a store that sells a specific product in a take-it-or-leave-it manner. The implicit justification for this situation is that existing services are fully utilized and resources are limited. Therefore, why should a move be made beyond the status quo? The obvious response is that "full demand" for services does not necessarily represent an optimal arrangement of services, and in fact may represent stagnation.[16] Clearly the needs of minorities can easily be overlooked when this situation prevails.

Nevertheless, the inescapable fact remains that community mental health practices cannot meet the needs of a diverse citizenry without understanding their values, beliefs, and behaviors. Information should be sought actively that helps fashion more responsive mental health services, and strategies for this purpose are discussed in chapters five, six, and seven. This process of information gathering should not be considered a job for someone else to do. Instead, this activity must be an integral part of the community mental health evaluation process. In this way, the constellation of services and the content of interventions will reflect real community concerns, as opposed to organizational constraints. This inquiry should start with a perusal of basic culture-linked issues. A brief synopsis of these is presented below.

Each cultural group has a belief system about mental illness, and this must be grasped. Because of the internal complexity found in ethnic populations, a better description is that multiple belief systems exist. Simply put, immigrants may tend to hold one view of mental illness, whereas the highly acculturated members of the same ethnic group may have a distinctive set of beliefs. An illustrative case is found in the pioneering work of Karno and Edgerton,[17] who discovered that Mexican Americans are unlikely to use mental health services, and are more likely than non-Hispanic whites to blur the distinction between somatic and mental health symptoms. Mexican Americans who are minimally acculturated are more likely to believe that the origins of mental health problems are organic, seek treatment from private physicians, and believe in the inheritability of mental illness to a far greater extent than native-born Mexican Americans or non-Hispanic whites. However, practitioners should also be aware that ethnic beliefs about mental illness are synergistic rather than static or "pure" types, and clients are fully capable of holding multiple perspectives that sometimes appear to be inconsistent.

Usually the essential point conveyed about acculturation is that a bifurcation exists between cultural traits based on ethnicity. However, a more apt portrayal is that ethnicity portends a difference in the concentration of beliefs and other qualitative factors. Various historical, social, and personal characteristics tend to influence the extent to which individual members of an ethnic group are committed to one belief system or another. For example, immigrants from Southeast Asia who are well educated and wealthy will probably not hold the same beliefs as individuals who are minimally educated and low income, despite a common national origin. There are also important cohort differences that should be recognized, as illustrated by the profound differences between those immigrants who arrived in the United States immediately after the revolution in Cuba and those who immigrated during the Mariel exodus in 1980. Despite the reality of common national origins, the two cohorts of immigrants had widely divergent social values and political beliefs, and this situation has impaired the social acceptance of the Mariel group in the original Cuban enclave in Miami.[18]

The role of the pluralistic practitioner should be to tap the range of beliefs present in a community, as well as those held by patients. Unfortunately few practitioners have been trained to collect this information. Comas-Diaz states that "ethnocultural assessments," using a protocol such as the one she has developed, are a therapeutic tool that "can help the patient manage cultural values, negotiate transitional experiences, and cope with the identity readjustment in an alien cultural environment."[19]

Parenthetically, Levine and Padilla point out that the effective therapist "assists clients to interpret their emotional problems in terms of their world view."[20] Indeed, social factors such as gender roles, social inequalities, and racism may be directly related to the personal distress and interpersonal conflicts of clients. But if practitioners are not "tuned-in" to a client's social situation, these points are likely to be submerged as a result of dealing only with presenting complaints and the diagnostic process.

Once this conceptual maneuver is made and cultural information becomes a part of the routine assessment process, various questions that are often ignored are suddenly elevated in importance.[21] For example, how and when are the signs or symptoms of mental incompetence perceived as illness and considered to warrant intervention? What role do cultural factors play in determining whether specific behaviors are viewed as deviant or signal the presence of a disease? Under what circumstances do family members and informal networks begin to influence this process? What are the cultural attitudes and role expectations toward those who are mentally ill, or about retaining them in the home?

In addition, information about folk beliefs may be important, especially if folk healers are widely used. Some community mental health providers have actually employed folk healers in order to learn more about the style and content of their beliefs and practices, as well as to address the psychiatric needs of patients who interpret their symptoms within a supernatural context. The record of such clinical practices is checkered. Some writers report success, while others describe serious problems in integrating the organic style of folk healers into formal treatment protocol.[22] The persistence of folk beliefs and the holistic orientation of many cultural minorities regarding the fusion of mind, body and soul, are well documented.[23] Folk beliefs must be taken into account in treating individuals who hold these views. On the other hand, a practitioner should never presume that all minority group members are equally committed to these precepts. Yet when such beliefs are present and ignored, as frequently occurs with recently immigrated Southeast Asians, services and therapists will be rejected.[24]

Furthermore, folk healers, do not necessarily compete with other mental health providers. Many patients patronize both, and see no conflict between these caregivers because they are thought to address distinct domains and satisfy quite different needs. Overall, despite some important exceptions, mental health providers have failed to take seriously folk beliefs and nontraditional practitioners.

The most regrettable stance, taken by some mental health professionals, is to regard folk beliefs as regressive and an obstacle to be overcome in the treatment process. Under these circumstances, the therapeutic mission is to change the views of clients, so that they will accept the clinical perspective of the therapist. Ultimately, clients are belittled. Perhaps the most perplexing aspect of this issue is that minority mental health practitioners are often the most resistant to accepting or incorporating folk beliefs into treatment plans, perhaps because they are sensitive to the negative connotations associated with these beliefs within the dominant culture, including among fellow mental health professionals.

The controversy surrounding the cultural acceptability of services has plagued the community mental health movement from its inception. This issue is related to the discussion of folk practices, but not because practitioners must masquerade as folk healers. Rather, mental health practitioners have failed, in many instances, to understand the expectations that clients have about treatment. Among many immigrant groups from third world countries, mental health services were never before available. Therefore, they find the typical diagnostic and treatment procedure perplexing and unsatisfying, and this is reflected in extraordinary levels of termination, especially after only one clinical visit.[25] Moreover, most people coming from a traditional culture attach a stigma to mental illness, and therefore they are very reluctant to seek help. Parenthetically, family members of disordered persons often hesitate to bring them in for treatment, because of the belief that the illness reflects badly on the family and the ability of its members to take care of their own problems. These cultural definitions and behaviors, in the context of a static provider system that depends on walk-in business, results in the systematic exclusion of many minority group members from the services delivery process.

Related to all of these issues is the general failure of the community health movement to instill, as a primary condition, a thoroughgoing desire to incorporate the element of culture into interventions. Obvious problems, related to the lack of bilingual and bicultural staff to serve linguistically diverse cultural groups, can be solved in time with the proper resources. However, the more subtle aspects of cultural sensitivity require an approach that is grounded in an appreciation of the integrity, continuity, and legitimacy of culture. This is an important point, because practitioners can easily be recruited who have linguistic fluency, but have not formed the requisite attitudes and knowledge base necessary to work effectively with cultural minorities. This is a recurring problem in community mental health, because most of the training received by professionals continues to stress clinical protocol over cultural awareness. The result is a "we-they" bifurcation between practitioners and community members, which prevents minorities from utilizing and benefiting from services. For example,

Levine and Padilla report that Mexican Americans have a favorable attitude about the intent of mental health services, perhaps even more so than non-Hispanic whites, but that they are dissuaded from using these services because the content is deemed unsuitable.

The notion of cultural sensitivity, in the broadest sense, refers to an awareness of the conscious and subconscious attributes shared by members of an ethnic group. Although such attributes are found in all human groups, they have an unique interpretation in each ethnic group.[26] As different groups confront a similar problem, each one finds a unique way of managing this issue, for example, mental illness and its sequelae. These cultural expressions are introduced through formal and informal socialization and, quite important, are the results of utilizing linguistic codes to create a medium for interpreting behaviors and emotions. For example, an "ataque de nervios," as witnessed in Puerto Rican culture (and other Latin American cultures as well), is an expression of distress, which is often precipitated by stressful life situations.[27] For mental health practitioners a common pitfall is to interpret the symptoms of an "ataque" within a formal diagnostic framework, thereby reaching a confounded diagnosis, as well as failing to comprehend the cultural significance of this "cry for help." The "ataque de nervios" represents a set of learned behaviors that are usually not found in the symptom presentation of non-Hispanic white patients.

The social subconscious is also affected, as noted by Levi-Strauss, since the imposition of cultural expectations on basic needs and drives creates a constant interplay of ideation, emotions, and imagery.[28] Resulting conflicts are imbued with cultural implications. For example, being a male homosexual in Latin American culture is so socially and culturally problematic that a complex panorama of intrapsychic and behavioral manifestations can be expected to accompany this situation. Material objects, symbols, and valued traditions also take on a sacred meaning through their ritualistic use in everyday life. Mental health practitioners should appreciate this information and incorporate it into interventions. Therefore, both the material and the nonmaterial domains should be the focus of attention, including their social and psychological ramifications. Failure to comprehend these subtleties has led mental health practitioners to view clients regularly as having a "cultural problem," which can be solved if these patients can be resocialized into more enlightened ways of thinking about their lives. Misunderstanding can also lead to the "category fallacy." This means clients are identified as having specific psychiatric disorders, because of the observational limitations of a diagnostic process that fails to incorporate culturally meaningful information.[29]

Cultural sensitivity implies the ability to penetrate the symbolic layers of meaning with careful observation and interpretation. Attaining this sensitivity requires both a proper method and an appropriate frame of reference. In this regard, Chavez recounts a case involving a twenty-eight-year-old Hispanic women who:

> is supporting her parents and extended family, was diagnosed as having a "mother" complex and attempting to emulate her father's role and become a husband to her mother or the adult men and women who, in accordance with their culture, remain in the family home until married, yet are diagnosed by Anglo therapists as "sheltered" or "passive-dependent."[30]

Clearly, this client's situation has been seriously misconstrued.

Another common foible in the mental health evaluation and planning process is that a client's *Lebensraum* is not adequately considered in the identification of either "risk" or access points for intervention. Although, in a strictly formal sense, risk groups can be pinpointed from epidemiologic and treatment data, these sources of information provide limited understanding of the sociocultural processes that underlie proneness for risk. Nevertheless, risk groups often represent aggregations of individuals who share life styles that have impact on the formation and maintenance of self-image and emotional stability. Unlocking this process requires more than knowledge about sociodemographic factors and diagnoses, although this may be a reasonable starting point. Because an epidemiologically identified risk group supplies only the parameters for investigating rather than explicating specific social processes, a culturally viable *modus operandi* for intervention should be established.

Often, children of immigrants experience high levels of psychological distress related to acculturation but merely examining epidemiologic markers will not offer much insight into this problem. In fact, culturally sensitive clinical studies have revealed that individuals who are unable to meet their personal needs within the context of one cultural setting, such as the family, may prefer or feel compelled to form other intimate social relationships, as may be found in peer groups. Although each group may be satisfying a deeply felt need of the individual, there may also be resulting conflicts. Because the individual is placed in a position of marginality with regard to his or her family of origin, the conventional sources for emotional support and social control are not available. This opens the door for the formation of a synthetic self-image and life style that may have serious social and emotional consequences. Attempting to achieve adaptive socialization and reformulate such a complex cultural field can lead to the destruction of what Aaron Antonovsky calls "cognitive coherence," or, stated differently, the manifestation of behaviors such as alcohol and drug use.[31]

Yet practitioners should be wary not to confuse cultural sensitivity with the adoption of stereotypes. Often experts are consulted, in order to develop "informed" profiles of various minority groups. However, sometimes these descriptions are not based on sound research. Regularly statements are made about "macho" Latin American males, for example, which might as well be derived from the popular press. While cultural regularities are certainly present, they have multiple dimensions.[32] Therefore, simplistic explanations or descriptions should not be uncritically accepted. Instead, attention should be directed to grasping how these patterns are created and sustained. Incorporating "seemingly" relevant images into an intervention may be more damaging than general insensitivity.

Facts about cultural minorities should not be accepted too literally without fully understanding their provisional nature. A relevant insight made by Weeks and Cuellar is that elderly Mexican Americans are as likely as Asians to acknowledge the importance of family bonds and the need for reciprocity. But, whereas the Asian elderly express a willingness to seek help from their children should they require assistance, older Mexican Americans are very reluctant to do so. The reason for this discrepancy is that Mexican American elderly are also committed to self-reliance, and within their normative framework becoming a "burden" is considered to be demeaning. Conversely, among Asians the "burden" placed on children represents expected "reciprocity behavior." Although the expressed values in the two groups regarding intrafamilial ties are similar, these beliefs are manifested in very different ways.[33]

Organizational Factors and Cultural Insensitivity

The same forces that lead to the medicalization of psychiatry have provoked a similar paradigm shift in the administration of mental health services. As noted by Greene:

> Probably more than any other array of health services, the structure of the mental health system has been defined by economic and financing issues. Understanding it to a very large degree, rests with the analysis of its administrative history and an explanation of its administrative requirements.[34]

Once federal support for community mental health services disintegrated and deinstitutionalization became haphazard, the face of CMHCs changed drastically. High caseloads saturated with chronic patients created a crisis for CMHCs, and many staff members were wholly unprepared for the resulting role implications. This change provides little flexibility for practitioners to experiment with community intervention. Moreover, payment mechanisms virtually require that traditional clinical settings be maintained. For example, typically a patient is required to have a DSM-III diagnosis to justify treatment, and only a traditional therapeutic consultation will satisfy the requirement for service reimbursement.

Perhaps the most significant new development is the emphasis on creating a new private marketplace for mental health services, in the belief that the private sector is better equipped to provide intervention and live within budget constraints. Indeed, some experts predict that in the near future private sector agencies will replace a majority of the programs that are currently available, despite the fact that payment for services will still come from public revenues.

Most likely, the privatization of mental health care will follow the medicalization path. The possibility for increasing cultural sensitivity or community interventions within this scenario is negligible. What will motivate private providers to become interested in minority culture or the empowerment of the minority community? Also it should be kept in mind that members of minority groups are least likely to have health insurance that will cover care, should they fail to qualify for services under regular reimbursement guidelines. And since mental health services utilization is particularly sensitive to the availability of third-party payment, this lack of insurances should attenuate minority utilization and reduce the quality of the services available to these persons.

Even CMHCs, which were created to deal with the common man, are quickly remodeling their operations to emulate health maintenance organizations and are increasingly looking for clients who can pay for services. Additionally, few of the newer providers in the "privatization" movement are creating facilities that are intended for use by indigent clients. As a result, for example, in many states the homeless and migrant workers, although technically qualifying for services, will not experience continuity of care because the delivery system is not designed to maintain these individuals as part of a practitioner's active caseload. This kind of regular involvement is simply too costly for private entrepreneurs to fund.

Despite the fact that the National Institute of Mental Health stills pays lip service to the goals of community mental health movement, little research is directed toward these serious economic policy issues that affect the quality and quantity of services received by minorities. In effect, the federal government has abdicated its role in providing leadership for true community intervention, due to the failure to propose compatible funding mechanisms that do not discourage the use of services. Additionally, despite the rapidly increasing social problems evident in urban America, which disproportionately affect minority communities, interventions that are based on social change and personal empowerment of minorities have been derailed. The reason for this practice is that they are considered politically undesirable and, therefore, "unscientific" and no bureaucratic or economic formula exists for their financial support.

Transcultural Training and Intervention

Due in part to the very rudimentary state of the transcultural training received by mental health professionals and to the absence of a paradigm for better understanding diverse cultural minorities, the community mental health movement has not developed the action model required to facilitate cross-cultural intervention. For example, in a study of minority content in clinical psychology training programs, Bernal and Padilla found that only a handful of programs required a sociocultural course for the Ph.D.[35] Indeed, although the number of minority graduate students is slightly increasing, the minority population is growing at such a rate its needs will not likely be met by minority practitioners.[36] Furthermore, as already noted, simply being a minority practitioner does not assure cross-cultural competence.

In order to develop the requisite knowledge base, community mental health professionals must move away from a strict reliance on intrapsychic models of intervention and treatment, and gain "an awareness of any factors that might limit the utility of existing counseling theories and approaches with any or all racial/ethnic minority groups."[37] Furthermore, practitioners should conceptualize minority help seeking as a process, rather than the result of the appearance of a condition.

Valle has described the elements necessary for the development of what he terms "cross-cultural competence." These include:

1. a working knowledge of the symbolic and linguistic "communicational" patterns of the target ethnic minority group(s);
2. knowledge and skill in relating to the naturalistic/interactional processes of the target population; and

3. a grasp of the underlying attitude, value, and belief systems of the target population.[38]

He adds that mental health practitioners have advocated in the past what Rothman et al. have called "spontaneous" change.[39] Presumed is that practitioners can put forward "some knowledge relevant to the target populations and then hope that cross-cultural competencies will emerge as serendipitous outcomes of the effort." This approach has been demonstrated historically to be a dismal failure for generating either a reliable information base or a training model for transcultural mental health intervention.

Valle also notes that a more systematic approach should cut across the life-styles of cultural minorities, without muting the significance of intragroup cultural variation. To that end, he has identified three dimensions for a cross-cultural competency model in mental health. These include: (1) socioeconomic and sociodemographic domains that provide a structural basis for lifestyle, such as occupational roles, familial configuration, educational status, etc.; (2) socioculturally expressed behaviors, including normative expectations, language usage, and interactional patterns; and, (3) acculturative levels that are identified as "traditional," "bicultural," and "assimilated." These dimensions are seen as dynamic and interactive, and provide the basis for a conceptual "road map" for understanding linguistically diverse minority communities, including the factors that contribute to mental disorder, help seeking behavior, and the selection of interventions. However, these dimensions should not be understood piecemeal. They should be linked together in sufficient detail, so that the intricacies of social process can be discerned.

The development of cross-cultural competence also requires that attention be given to important sources of division and social change within cultural groups. For example, there is an extensive literature on intracultural and intergenerational variation among immigrant groups, stress of acculturation, and how family dysfunction is linked to differential levels of acculturation.[40] Cultural minority groups that contain a large percentage of immigrants cannot be adequately appreciated without understanding the implications of acculturation and related processes, especially in the context of poverty as well as the unique problems faced by refugees. Immigrants must overcome a host of challenges in adapting to their new environment, such as coming to terms with a lack of interpersonal ties and dealing with cultural change and the social mobility of their children. Decades ago Margaret Mead discussed these issues while noting that the problems of immigrant parents and their children are very different, and that perhaps the children are the ones who ultimately confront the greater challenge and higher risk for maladaption. The research of Szapocznik and his colleagues tends to confirm this view. In the case of Cuban Americans, for example, differences in acculturation levels between male children and their parents are a good predictor of family conflicts and adolescent drug use.[41] The traditional community mental health approach of dealing with individuals often bypasses these essential family relationships, which are of vital importance for effective treatment.

Mental health practitioners must be sensitive to how each immigrant group reestablishes networks and enclaves, in order to provide cultural continuity, integration, and social support for its members. Networks and social support also have been widely studied, thereby revealing that interactional networks exist on many levels and for many purposes.[42] Historically, community mental health practitioners have avoided dealing with these informal groups, although they are potentially the most important resource for understanding and intervening in minority communities.[43] The reasons for this omission are multiple. Despite the existence of an enormous amount of literature, little contemporary research has been devoted to the comparative assessment of interactional networks. Therefore, although these networks are known to exist, practitioners do not know how to locate them, how to differentiate them in terms of their purpose or membership, or how to enter them.

This situation is truly ironic, since the original premise of the community mental health movement was to engage the community. However, "engaging" the community has come to mean physically setting up shop in minority neighborhoods, and making contacts with prominent community leaders and other human services agency personnel. While strategies are available for mapping social networks in minority communities, they have rarely been studied seriously in graduate schools or operationalized by practitioners. There is no doubt that this type of work is labor intensive, but making a concerted effort to understand community networks and intervene in them could revolutionize the focus of services. Moreover, interactional networks should be of central importance in the training of practitioners who are culturally sensitive. These networks provide a basis for understanding cultural beliefs, norms, and behaviors. Also supplied is a blueprint for comprehending help seeking processes and for providing endogenous treatment of the mentally ill.

Most practitioners are trained in a limited way and implement the techniques they have learned even if these strategies have little relevance to cultural minorities. The present minimal evaluation of treatment efficacy allows this situation to continue unabated. This dereliction is often justified by the statement, "You can't measure what I do." Conversely, no one is measuring what is not happening. Considering the propensity to uphold the status quo and to favor familiar interventions, community approaches have trouble getting started.

Yet, practitioners who are wed to acultural intervention models and perspectives are readily able to belittle or misconstrue cultural arrangements and practices. Furthermore, the history of the community mental health movement indicates that many therapists never accepted the substantive implications of community involvement, which would have required inserting themselves into both the culture and politics of communities. Practitioners have found the political arena to be especially problematic, because the content of their training, their professional self-image, and potential role conflict have increasingly operated as powerful disincentives to engaging in activism. After all, the idea that a practitioner should be a community reformer was fashioned during a period when human service workers were expected to be advocates of political change.[44] Today, activism is no longer considered to be a legitimate function of mental health workers. Real community involvement is viewed as "too far out" and a threat to the clinical services model. Furthermore, the increasing emphasis on chronic mental illness and funding reductions have forced services back into a traditional clinical mode.

All of this has created what Chavez calls a "collision of mission," because CMHCs were "founded on principles established in the 1960's staffed with people educated in the 1970's to deal with the mental health realities of the 1980's."[45] Even many practitioners who have attempted to go against the grain, and work with community intervention models, face an enormous burden because community expertise and activism are oftentimes neither supported nor rewarded.

Conclusion: The Need for Direct Intervention

Obviously this situation cannot continue. Social conditions have worsened in urban areas, while immigration has changed the landscape of many American cities. During the past eight years poverty has increased while drug and other problems have proliferated. While all this was going on, service delivery became increasingly conservative. Yet this inaction can no longer be tolerated, if an increasing segment of the population is to have any hope of a productive life.

Leaving problems alone and hoping that they will disappear is clearly an ill-conceived policy. Deleterious social conditions will abate only through active intervention. But traditional correctives are not the answer.

The mental health system is currently bureaucratic and wasteful, not to mention completely divorced from the source of problems. Accordingly, maybe the time has come to resurrect the philosophical core of the community mental health movement, for this orientation offers an opportunity for timely, relevant, and effective interventions. In order to avoid repeating the mistakes of the past, however, a complete overhaul of methods for community intervention is necessary. Addressed in the following chapter will be several conceptual and methodological issues associated with the delivery of mental health services that can assist in the process of restructuring community mental health.

Notes

1. Kirmayer, Laurence. "Culture, Affect, and Somatization—Part II," *Transcultural Psychiatry Review* 21(2), 1984, pp. 237–262; Kleinman, Arthur. "Depression, Somatization and the 'New Cross-Cultural Psychiatry,' " *Social Science and Medicine* 11(1), 1977, pp. 3–10.

2. Link, Bruce and Bruce Dohrenwend. "Formulation of Hypotheses About the True Prevalence of Demoralization in the United States." In *Mental Illness in the United States: Epidemiologic Estimates*, ed. Bruce P. Dohrenwend, Barbara S. Dohrenwend, M. Goved, et al. (New York: Praeger, 1980).

3. Klerman, Gerald L. "Psychiatric Diagnostic Categories: Illness of Validity and Measurement," *Journal of Health and Social Behavior* 30(1), 1989, pp. 26–32.

4. Mirowsky, John and Catherine E. Ross. "Psychiatric Diagnosis as Reified Measurement," *Journal of Health and Social Behavior* 30(1), 1989, pp. 11–25.

5. Srole, Leo and Anita K. Fisher. "Debate on Psychiatric Epidemiology," *Archives of General Psychiatry* 37(12), 1980, pp. 1421–1423.

6. Tweed, Dan L. and Linda K. George. "A More Balanced Perspective on 'Psychiatric Diagnosis as Reified Measurement,' " *Journal of Health and Social Behavior* 30(1), 1989, pp. 35–37.

7. Cockerham, William. *Medical Sociology*. (Englewood Cliffs, NJ: Prentice-Hall, 1989).

8. Kleinman, Arthur. *The Illness Narrative*. (New York: Basic Books, 1988).

9. Karson, Craig N., Joel E. Kleinman, Richard Jed Wyatt. "Biochemical Concepts of Schizophrenia." In *Contemporary Directions in Psychopathology: Toward the DSM-IV*, ed. Theodore Millon and Gerald L. Klermon. (New York: Guilford Press, 1986), pp. 495–518.

10. Mechanic, David. *Mental Health and Social Policy*. (Englewood Cliffs, NJ: Prentice-Hall, 1989).

11. Karno, Marvin, Janis H. Jenkins, Aurora de la Salva, Felipe Santana, Cynthia Telles, Steven Lopez, and Jim Mintz. "Expressed Emotion and Schizophrenic Outcome Among Mexican-American Families," *Journal of Nervous and Mental Disease* 175(3), 1987, pp. 143–151.

12. Regier, Darrel A., Irving D. Goldberg, and Carl A. Toube. "The de Facto U.S. Mental Health Services System: A Public Health Perspective," *Archives of General Psychiatry* 35(6), 1978, pp. 685–693.

13. Hough, Richard L., John A. Lanswerk, Marvin Karno et al. "Utilization of Health and Mental Health Services by Los Angeles Mexican Americans and Non-Hispanic Whites," *Archives of General Psychiatry* 44(8), 1987, pp. 702–709.

14. Kleinman, *The Illness Narrative*, pp. 252–267.

15. Kolody, Bohdon, William Vega, Kenneth Meinhardt, and Gloria Dennissen. "The Correspondence of Health Complaints and Depressive Symptoms Among Anglos and Mexican Americans," *Journal of Nervous and Mental Disease* 174(4), 1986, pp. 221–228.

16. Meinhardt, Kenneth and William Vega. "A Method for Estimating Underutilization of Mental Health Services by Ethnic Groups," *Hospital and Community Psychiatry* 38(11), 1987, pp. 1186–1190.

17. Karno, Marvin and Robert B. Edgerton. "Perception of Mental Illness in a Mexican American Community," *Archives of General Psychiatry* 20(2), 1969, pp. 233–238.

18. Camayd-Freixas, Yohel. *Crisis in Miami*. (Boston: Boston Urban Research and Development Group, 1988).

19. Comas-Diaz, Lillian. "Cross-Cultural Mental Health Treatment." In *Clinical Guidelines in Cross-Cultural Mental Health*, ed. Lillian Comas-Diaz and Ezra E. H. Griffith. (New York: John Wiley and Sons, 1988), pp. 337–361.

20. Levine, E. S. and Amado M. Padilla. *Crossing Cultures in Therapy: Pluralistic Counseling for the Hispanic*. (Monterey, CA: Brooks/Cole, 1980), p. 264.

21. Snowden, Lonnie R. "Toward Evaluation of Block Psycho Social Competence." In *The Pluralistic Society*, ed. Stanley Sue and Thom Moore. (New York: Human Science Press, 1984), pp. 179–201; Geller, Jesse D. "Racial Bias in the Evaluation of Patients for Psychotherapy." In *Clinical Guidelines in Cross-Cultural Mental Health*, ed. Lillian Comas-Diaz and Ezra E. H. Griffith. (New York: John Wiley and Sons, 1988), pp. 112–134.

22. Ruiz, Pedro and John Langrod. "The Role of Folk Healers in Community Mental Health Services," *Community Mental Health Journal* 12(6), 1976, pp. 392–404; Torrey, E. F. "The Core for the Indigenous Therapist," *Archives in General Psychiatry* 20(3), 1969, pp. 365–373; Lefley, Harriet P. "Delivering Mental Health Services Across Cultures." In *Mental Health Services: The Cross-Cultural Context*, ed. Paul B. Pedersen, Norman Sartorius and Anthony J. Marsella. (Beverly Hills, CA: Sage, 1984), pp. 135–171.

23. Sandoval, Mercedes C. "Santeria: Afro-Cuban Concepts of Disease and Its Treatment in Miami," *Journal of Operational Psychiatry* 8(2), 1977, pp. 52–65; Trotter, R. and J. Charina. *Curanderismo: The Gift of Healing*. (Athens, GA: University of Georgia Press, 1982).

24. Bliatout, Bruce T., Rath Ben, Vinh T. Do, Kham O. Deopraseuth, Hollis Y. Bliatout, and David T.-T. Lee. "Mental Health and Prevention Activities Targeted to Southeast Asian Refugees." In *Southeast Asian Mental Health: Treatment, Prevention, Services, Training, and Research*, ed. Tom C. Owon. (Rockville, MD: National Institute of Mental Health, 1985), pp. 183–207.

25. Sue, Stanley and Nolan Zane. "Therapists' Credibility and Giving: Implications for Practice and Training in Asian-American Communities." In *Mental Health Research*

and Practices in Minority Communities, ed. Manuel Miranda and Harry H. Kitano. (Rockville, MD: National Institute of Mental Health, 1986), pp. 157–167.

26. Lefley, Harriet P. "Self-Perception and Primary Prevention." In *New Directions in Prevention Among American Indians and Alaska Native Communities*, ed. Spero M. Mouron. (Portland, OR: Oregon Health Science University, 1982), pp. 65–90.

27. Guarnaccia, Peter J., Maritza Rubio-Stipec, and Glorisa Canino. "Ataques de Nervios in the Puerto Rican Diagnostic Interview Schedule: The Import of Cultural Categories on Psychiatric Epidemiology," *Culture, Medicine, and Psychiatry* 13(3), 1989, pp. 275–295.

28. Levi-Strauss, Claude. *Structural Anthropology*. (New York: Basic Books, 1963).

29. Good, Byron and Mary-Jo Good. "The Cultural Context of Diagnosis and Therapy: A View From Medical Anthropology." In *Mental Health Research and Practice in Minority Communities*, ed. Manuel Miranda and Harry H. Kitano. (Rockville, MD: National Institute of Mental Health, 1986), pp. 1–25.

30. Chavez, Nelba. "Mental Health Services Delivery to Minority Populations: Hispanics—A Perspective." In *Mental Health Research and Practice in Minority Communities: Development of Culturally Sensitive Training Programs*, ed. Manuel Miranda and Harry H. Kitano. (Rockville, MD: National Institute of Mental Health, 1986), pp. 145–156.

31. Szapoczick, Jose, P. Daruna, M. Scopetta, and M. Aranalde. "The Characteristics of Cuban Immigrant Inhalant Abusers," *American Journal of Drug and Alcohol Abuse* 4(3), 1977, pp. 377–389.

32. Ybarra, Lea. "When Wives Work: The Impact on the Chicano Family," *Journal of Marriage and the Family* 44(1), 1982, pp. 169–178.

33. Weeks, John and Jose Cuellar. "The Role of Family Members in the Helping Networks of Older People," *Gerontologist* 21(4), 1981, pp. 388–394.

34. Greene, Barry R. "Evolving Mental Health Policy: Implications for Health Administration," *Journal of Health Administration Education* 2(2), Spring 1984, pp. 193–220.

35. Bernal, Martha E. and Amado M. Padilla. "Status of Minority Curricula and Training in Clinical Psychology," *American Psychologist* 37(7), 1982, pp. 780–787.

36. Bernal, Martha E. "Hispanic Issues in Psychology: Curricula and Training," *Hispanic Journal of Behavioral Sciences* 2(2), 1980, pp. 129–146.

37. Casas, Manuel. "Making Effective Use of Research to Impact the Training of Culturally Sensitive Mental Health Workers." In *Mental Health Research and Practice in Minority Communities*, ed. Manuel Miranda and Harry H. Kitano. (Rockville, MD: National Institute of Mental Health, 1986), pp. 117–132.

38. Valle, Ramon. "Cross-cultural Competence in Minority Communities: A Curriculum Implementation Strategy." In *Mental Health Research and Practice in Minority Communities*, ed. Manuel Miranda and Harry H. Kitano. (Rockville, MD: National Institute of Mental Health, 1986), pp. 29–50.

39. Rothman, J., J. L. Erlich, and J. Teresa. "Adding Something New: Innovation." In *Tactics and Techniques of Community Practice*, ed. F. M. Cox, J. L. Erlich, J. Rothman, and J. E. Tropman. (Itaska, IL: Peacock Publishing, 1977).

40. Mindel, Charles H., Robert W. Habenstein, and Roosevelt Wright (eds.). *Ethnic Families in America*. (New York: Elseuier, 1983); Powell, Gloria (ed.). *The Psychosocial Development of Minority Group Children*. (New York: Brunner-Mazel, 1983).

41. Szapocznik, Jose and William Kurtines. "Acculturation, Biculturism and Adjustment Among Cuban Americans." In *Psychological Dimensions on the Acculturation Process: Theory, Models, and Some New Findings*, ed. Amado Padilla. (Boulder, CO: Westview, 1979).

42. Cohen, Samuel and Leonard Syme. *Social Support and Health.* (New York: Academics Press, 1984); Lin, Nan, Alfred Dean, and Walter M. Ensel (eds.). *Social Support, Life Events, and Depression.* (Orlando, FL: Academic Press, 1986).

43. Caplan, Gerold and Marie Killilea (eds.). *Support Systems and Mental Help.* (New York: Grune and Stratton, 1976).

44. Wagenfeld, Morton and Stanley S. Robin. "Social Activism and Community Mental Health: A Policy Perspective," *Administration in Mental Health* 8(1), 1980, pp. 31–45.

45. Chavez, "Mental Health Services Delivery to Minority Populations: Hispanics—A Perspective," p. 151.

Chapter Five

Reconceptualizing Knowledge, Order, Illness, and Intervention

Introduction

Unless the general purpose of public mental health care is going to be abandoned, key elements of service delivery will have to be rethought. In fact, the potential constituency eligible for services from public health practitioners is expanding. That is, the groups that do not have access to private clinics are becoming more numerous and culturally varied. If a community-based approach to intervention is not inaugurated, this population will not likely receive adequate services. Intervention may eventually consist of nothing more than the administration of medication ("meds"), occasionally in a haphazard manner, for the purpose of controlling momentarily a volatile individual or situation. Accordingly, treatment that actually promotes both individual and collective empowerment, one of the original goals of the community mental health movement, may never be achieved.

As noted earlier, community-based intervention should be underpinned by a nondualistic orientation. The traditional intervention "loop," therefore, should be reevaluated in view of this new philosophy.[1] Yet this shift in thinking does not require that every traditional procedure be jettisoned, or that intervention be limited to a few specific practices. Instead, it should be recognized at each stage of intervention that knowledge is framed by the questions posed by clients and practitioners. Gathering knowledge and prescribing practical solutions for problems are thus not necessarily scientific but cultural activities, as will be illustrated in chapter six.

Intervention should be directed to the nexus of interhuman relationships. This is the dimension that unites persons, and is where norms, roles, and other social artifacts are stored. Clearly this realm is not static, but is altered constantly by a host of factors. As new groups and novel forms of discourse enter the social patchwork, the dialogue that binds persons together changes. What this means is that "communicative competence" is difficult but not impossible to acquire.[2] Furthermore, gaining this sort of competence is not achieved once and for all. As Edmund Husserl suggests, practitioners who are not going to be considered naive should always initiate an intervention as "beginners."[3]

Husserl's point is that wonder (*thaumazein*) is vital to a successful intervention. Earlier this activity was referred to as "reflexivity." When practitioners are not enamored of assumptions, each client evaluation or needs assessment can begin anew. Stale and outmoded methods do not have to be used, simply because they are considered to be traditional or scientific. Doubtless, flexibility is increased, because professional or bureaucratic mandates are unable to dictate the course of an intervention. The likelihood of a socially responsive intervention taking place is thus improved. Each problem along the so-called "continuum of treatment" can be identified in a culturally appropriate manner, with a contextually relevant remedy administered.

Clearly interventions that are insensitive to the existential texture of social reality are reductionistic. For the realm of the interhuman is polymorphic and resistant to simplistic explanations.[4] At this juncture a new phrase needs to be introduced, in order to illustrate vividly the social impact of reductionism. "Symbolic violence" is a notion popularized by Pierre Bourdieu, which captures adequately the debilitating effects of reductionistic practices.[5]

Often reductionism is interpreted to mean that knowledge is selectively acquired. As a result, attention is given to some information, while other sources of input are ignored. The upshot of reductionism is generally understood to be that a holistic analysis is not undertaken. But is this all that occurs? Is the key shortcoming of reductionism that the data collection process has parameters, and thus, by definition, certain areas of social life are excluded? If this were the case, every intervention would be reductionistic, even those that are ostensibly community-based. From a community-based perspective, however, the problem is not that knowledge procurement and diagnoses, for example, are finite, but that these activities may be based on socially irrelevant criteria. When this is the case, "symbolic violence" is perpetrated.

What is the upshot of symbolic violence? Most important, specific sources of knowledge, certain kinds of logic, and various types of information are discredited. As a result of providing particular data categories or explanations with a seignorial status, a host of other options are inadvertently undermined. Persons are urged, as Bourdieu says, to agree with the "destruction of their instruments of expression."[6] Information that does not fulfill specific requirements, which are often quite rarefied, is rejected. Obviously more is happening than providing simply a partial picture of a situation. Significantly more crucial is that a client's response may be undermined, because it is associated with irrational behavior. Clients may be required to deny legitimacy to their actions. In this way, the *meaning* of behavior is destroyed; the robustness of facts is truncated. Persons are thus treated as homunculi, who have little to say that is meaningful about their condition. In short, symbolic violence is tolerated because subverting the legitimacy of certain knowledge bases is not viewed as particularly problematic. Hence intervention can easily become the means, as is often the case, whereby various persons or groups are intimidated or dominated.

In order to avert this sort of violence—which may be even more devastating to personal functioning than a physical attack—a nondualistic intervention cycle is proposed. When approached as nondualistic, intervention strategies should be developed and brought to fruition within the web of discursive practices that constitute every aspect of reality. Any attempt to provide data collection methodologies or other clinical techniques with an exalted status is foiled, because the symbolic character of knowledge is difficult to rationalize away. Accordingly, when symbolic violence is avoided, both the self-presentation of clients and the social voice of facts can be revealed.

New Reasoning About Illness

In order to undertake a community-based intervention, the stigma that is usually attached to illness, particularly mental impairment, should be challenged. Avoiding stigmatization is particularly noteworthy in community sensitive interventions for two reasons. First, the community should be the focus of attention. Hence persons must be willing to become involved in identifying, preventing, and curing illness. As long as a stigma is attached to dealing directly with social problems, this activity will remain within the purview of professionals. Those who are integral to the success of community-based interventions, in short, will be reluctant to commit the necessary time and energy to these tasks.

Second, illness should be investigated on its own terms. But if illness is believed to be a manifestation of deviance, symbolic violence will most likely occur. Almost by definition, deviance does not have a positive identity. Indicated by deviance is a movement away from what is considered to be normal, positive, or fruitful. Therefore, whatever is assumed to be deviant is measured against reified behavioral expectations. Absolute standards of normalcy, in other words, are used to determine the nature of deviance. Examining what Schutz calls a "null point" is a substitution for studying real needs.[7]

This paradox is rooted in the dualism that pervades Western philosophy. Foucault argues correctly, for example, that reason and nonreason have been traditionally juxtaposed.[8] Further, reason and the absence of rationality occupy completely different realms. Reason is based on fundamental principles, from which all reasonable conclusions can be derived. The means and the expected outcome of an action are necessarily connected. This is not the case with nonrational behavior. As is most notably illustrated by Pareto, nonrational actions are idiosyncratic and unrelated to general and predictable explanatory themes.[9] "Non-logical actions originate chiefly in definite psychic states, sentiments, subconscious feelings, and the like."[10] What this means is that anything labelled nonrational is not assumed to follow rules. In sum, nonrational behavior is frenetic—means and ends are randomly related—and thus cannot be studied in a serious manner.

Obviously differentiating rationality from irrationality in this manner should be unacceptable to community-based practitioners. Particular styles of thinking, because they are generally accepted as rational, should not be permitted to dominate other approaches to conceptualizing reality. Because rationality and irrationality are linguistic determinations, no sound rationale is available to sustain this bifurcation. Rationality, stated simply, does not exist a priori. Madness and deviance, especially in the context of the cultural differences that may exist between a client and therapist, represent unique forms of reason, rather than the absence of rationality. Madness is indicative of a particular patois, rather than a breakdown of "*homo natura*."[11] Echoing this theme, Shoshana Felman writes that madness is the outcome of a unique style of writing, or expression, that does not have widespread acceptance.[12]

Subverting the rationality-irrationality distinction contributes significantly to the use of community-based interventions. Because nonreason is a matter of interpretation, the stigma regularly associated with madness or deviance can be eliminated. Becoming involved in interventions, therefore, should not be something for citizens to fear. Also, the way is prepared for the experience of mental illness to be studied, so this mode of organizing reality might be appreciated with regard to its cultural manifestations. The reality rather than the "myth of madness", in other words, is investigated. Clearly this should be the aim of community-based intervention.

Assessing the Needs of Culturally Diverse Communities

Usually the delivery of services begins with an assessment of need. Indeed, these services are useless, unless they are designed appropriately to correct a particular problem. Most practitioners would agree that intervention should not be haphazard. Untargeted services with global objectives, in short, are ineffective and uneconomical.

Although there is a tendency to assume that intervention is admirable, enthusiasm is not sufficient to determine where services should be directed. As a result, an entire field of program evaluation has emerged. And anyone who has had minimal acquaintance with evaluation research is aware of the extremely political and controversial nature of these activities. While both state and federal agencies have required that need assessments be undertaken before funds are allocated and projects are begun, this research is commonly known to consist of "quick and dirty" studies. Particularly during a period of budget retrenchment, indirect services, such as program evaluation and research, are the first to be reduced. Therefore, needs assessments are often conducted in the most expedient manner possible, and the resulting information is often used selectively to justify the already existing service modalities.

Often technical needs assessment strategies are adopted that consist of using mathematical models and other projection techniques, which identify the level of need based on routinely collected utilization information. For example, as a result of time-series analysis, the number of chronically mentally ill patients who will request treatment or be involuntarily committed in the coming years can be predicted from previous intake reports.[13] Furthermore, indicator models are available that use census data and ecological information, for example, quality of housing or crime rates, to determine how many mentally ill persons are likely to reside in a particular area. Even when "key informants" are contacted and interviewed, these individuals are routinely chosen because they possess certain ethnic traits, belong to visible organizations, or reside in particular neighborhoods.

What these technological assessments usually lack is a cultural component. On the basis of several environmental or sociodemographic characteristics, the needs of a community are estimated. Thus, according to Schutz, the motives of clients are constructed on the basis of an artificial environment.[14] At best, this procedure is dubious. Why should researchers assume that a prominent Hispanic official has extensive knowledge of the

"Hispanic community"? Although these persons are usually identified as key informants, they may not be "key citizens" in the community that is being studied.[15] In other words, their knowledge of pertinent issues may be limited or distorted.[16] Defining "risk" in terms of ecological variables is equally problematic. Being "at risk" is a process, rather than a static condition associated with specific traits. Therefore, at minimum, the way the environment is interpreted, the coping mechanisms adopted by persons, and a community's reaction to a particular issue must be known before an adequate determination of need can be assured.[17]

All technological strategies share a similar fallacy. Assumed in each case is that need can be extrapolated from a variety of observable characteristics. But how is this possible, for implied by the concept of need is that a particular condition has not yet been achieved? How can a desired life-style be known from examining statistics pertaining to the quality of housing? The present housing conditions may or may not be adequate! To apply a classic formulation, "ought" cannot be derived from what "is."[18] The only way to understand need is to know the goals of a community. These are not ideal goals which might be realized if a perfect society could be created, but represent the level of existence persons define as acceptable.

From a dualistic point of view, however, identifying need by referring to empirical properties is understandable. Why should a subjective projection be given any credence? For surely social needs can be assessed in a manner similar to any other physiological or natural property. Undoubtedly natural systems have a level of operation that must be maintained, or undesirable consequences will occur. So why not describe humans and communities in this way, with need representing a significant departure from the norm or disequilibrium?

In terms of community-based intervention, nonetheless, this model should not be applied to ascertain social needs. Simply put, a natural condition is assumed to exist, while need is portrayed as a deficiency. Need is thus unrelated to personal or collective desires, but is a condition that should be avoided. Instead of learning about need, the aim is to restore equilibrium. Similar to nonreason, need constitutes an absence or residual category. But, in the social sense, need is a positive force, for implied are conditions that must be met if life is going to be satisfying, along with behavior that may be exhibited if certain goals are not achieved. Obviously more insight is provided by this version of need than when this idea is defined as a deficient state.

The Character of Data

The broadest possible range of data should be utilized by community-based practitioners. Hence entrée can be gained into the multifaceted nature of social life. When data are allowed to proliferate, the chances are improved that reductionism and symbolic violence will be avoided. In other words, data collection can expand until the language game that is played in a particular location is penetrated and adequately translated.

This sort of translation, however, requires flexibility and creativity. But when data collection methodologies are adopted that are technologically oriented, rigidity is the result. For example, the kind of data that can be accepted as valid is restricted by the separation of fact from value. Data, in short, are supposed to be "hard" or unrelated to interpretation. When computers are introduced into the intervention process, and data processing requirements begin to dictate how knowledge is conceptualized, this situation becomes worse.[19] In short, only data with exact parameters—Dreyfus refers to this information as "disembodied"—are believed to have any utility.[20] As should be noted, this desire to appear precise has deleterious consequences for data selection and planning.

When technical precision is stressed instead of cultural sensitivity, for instance, clinical or social assessment tends to be equated with testing. Because of their standardized format, tests are expected to be objective and thus reliable. Furthermore, tests are treated as valid measures even though many practitioners realize this assumption is questionable. Indeed, even when tests are interpreted, statistical criteria are invoked for this purpose. As a result, data appear to have a life of their own, and the effects of interpretation are assumed to be minimized during testing. Again, data must be amenable to quantification, for example, or else they will not likely be given serious attention. All input must be verified by so-called objective sources, such as experts or experimental protocol.

Nonetheless, technical standards are not value-free, as Weber recognized quite some time ago.[21] Even technical criteria are sustained by tacitly held beliefs about knowledge and reality. And as is discussed in chapter three, these assumptions can subtly influence how data are chosen and analyzed. The problem with this methodology is that a vast amount of information is excluded from consideration.

Although technical assessment methods have obvious applications and are efficient, socially responsible planning is difficult when data selection is restricted in the manner required by these procedures. As a consequence of dualism, however, this exclusionary methodology is justified. Data are either subjective or objective, and, according to this topology, if they are subjective they must be "objectified." Why would anyone give credence to the opinions of an ordinary community resident, when procedures that are allegedly value free are available to collect information?

Yet no knowledge base or technique should be allowed to monopolize the search for information, for objectivity is not necessarily associated with a particular kind of data or methodology. In effect, a key repercussion of rejecting dualism is that the data collection process is democratized, due to the emergence of a wide range of knowledge bases.[22] Any methodology that is socially relevant can be tried, while the sources of data that are available for exploration are enlarged. When the principle of relevance, rather than objectivity, guides the acquisition of information, data collection can develop in ways that were formally treated as objectionable.

Particularly noteworthy is that the traditional conceptions of data are no longer sacrosanct. Questions about the quality of data acquire a social rather than a technological orientation. Therefore, no source of knowledge should be viewed automatically to supplement another. This is a social determination, which can be made only after many forms of data and methodologies have been reviewed. The use of multiple measures and unusual knowledge bases is thus encouraged.[23] Any maneuver that facilitates understanding a community's language game can be pursued. In this way, every possible step can be taken to engender "social competence" on the part of practitioners.

The Metaphysics of Intervention

The phrase "the metaphysics of intervention" refers to the fundamental imagery that sustains the accumulation and implementation of knowledge. Specified by this metaphysics is the way knowledge is conceptualized, in addition to the intervention tactics adopted by practitioners. Nowadays the theme of holism, for example, has become quite popular.[24] Holism assumes that knowledge bases should be integrated, reductionism should be avoided, and interventions should be variegated. Clearly community-based practitioners should agree with each of these ideas. The problem to be examined in this section pertains to whether or not the imagery that is operational today actually fosters holism.

Insuring a holistic analysis has not always had a high priority, and, in fact, this imagery has been discouraged by dualism.[25] Considering the dualistic proposal essential to empiricism, holism compromises the search for accurate knowledge. Facts are supposed to be independent, as is indicated by the traditional symbolism *A* equals *A*, *B* equals *B*, and *A* does not equal *B*. An empirical datum, in other words, has a single identity that can only be obscured by introducing situational and other extenuating circumstances. At best, facts are interdependent but are not necessarily interpenetrating or directly related. For assuming that variables are interrelated, for example, unduly complicates the discovery of cause-effect relationships. In order for *A* to lead to *B* ($A \rightarrow$ B), the identity of *A* cannot be convoluted.

As a result of this conventional imagery, both the natural and social worlds are portrayed as fragmented. Atomism, simply put, is perpetrated, for society is envisioned to consist of a host of concatenated realms. For example, the self is juxtaposed to the environment, while the mind is separated from the body. Additionally, even the thinking process is described nowadays by using computer metaphors, whereby ideas and emotions are thought to be distinct. In actual practice, this dualism is manifested in the separation of psychological and sociological factors.

Within the limitations imposed by dualism, there appeared to be no way to integrate the myriad of factors that contribute to the genesis of social phenomena. A less reductionistic mode of conceptualization, therefore, was sought.[26] One outgrowth of the disillusionment with dualism is systems theory. As is suggested by the term "system," each piece of information is believed to be a part of a much larger composite. All knowledge, in other words, is integrated to form an organic whole. Therefore, advocates of systems theory charge that the traditional fragmented analyses can be overcome by accepting this position.

Supporters of community-based intervention, however, should question whether dualism is avoided by systems theory. More to the point, is the part-whole rendition of dualism retained? Although the focus is shifted away from the individual, the whole is clearly reified. Because the whole is believed to be "greater than the sum of its parts," a system represents an autonomous unit.[27] This formulation of the part-whole relationship is cited by Sutherland to culminate in "macrodeterminacy."[28] Establishing control of the system, stated differently, is more important than maintaining the integrity of its units.

As a consequence of part-whole dualism, justification still appears to be present for fragmented and insensitive analyses. This problem is clearly evident in the "continuum of care" model that was adopted in California. As a result of viewing the intervention process to be a continuum, sensitivity and efficiency were thought to be improved. A comprehensive model was available that allowed each problem to be aligned with an appropriate treatment. Nonetheless, as with systems approaches in general, the primary focus was on insuring the internal consistency of the scheme; on guaranteeing that each subcomponent is consistent with higher order principles. Degrees of illness were identified, along with a full range of interventions. Hence fine distinctions could be made between impairment and functioning, thereby enabling patients to be placed in the "least restrictive environment."

Stressing consistency in this way, however, misdirected the focus of intervention. Simply put, little concern was exhibited pertaining to the diverse nature of the communities that were supposed to be serviced. Whether or not persons viewed the services as relevant, understood the pathways to treatment, or agreed with the clinical labels that were used was not of primary importance. Instead, the thrust was to produce a placement system with refined gradations. Overlooked, in sum, are the individual elements of a clinical scheme that should be given attention by a community-based intervention model.

Clearly, justification is also retained for giving primacy to particular types of knowledge when describing and organizing institutions. Throughout the application process, the effects of the dualism that pervade systems theory are visible. For instance, although decentralization has become a prominent theme, most social service agencies remain bureaucratic or abstract systems.[29] Accordingly, particular scientists, technical experts, or bureaucrats are regularly assigned the task of implementing policies. These officials are presumed to be dispassionate, rational, and thus objective, due to the exalted position they hold in the division of labor. While using systems theory to organize these agencies may improve institutional control, through the reduction of participation in organization affairs, the resulting social implications are questionable. In short, knowledge is centralized and unavailable for critique. Consequently, intervention is not truly socially or culturally grounded.

New imagery has been introduced by Jean Gebser to resolve this problem. Actually, his aim is to be nondualistic, and thus he refuses to call any phenomenon a system. For example, he contends that neither a clinical system nor an organization is structured as a monolithic unit, which has a clear and distinct center. Instead, every aspect of social life is comprised of disparate elements. These factors, moreover, are related directly on the basis of their differences. Through the *recognition of their differences*, which occurs as a part of both agreements and disagreements, a semblance of integration is preserved.[30] Thus he refers to an organization as a "systase," rather than a system.[31] A systase is not categorically different from its parts.

As a consequence of abandoning dualism, the hierarchy that accompanies systems theory cannot be justified. No reality *sui generis* is legitimate. Only direct integration has any validity. This new metaphysics that should be a part of community-based intervention, therefore, is predicated on the protection and integration, rather than the assimilation, of differences. What are the implications of this theoretical shift for intervention? Obviously the identification, collection, and utilization of knowledge are affected by this change.

First, facts are not independent but implicated in surrounding circumstances. The intricate nature of intervention is thus suggested. Second, rather than related logically, cause and effect are directly mediated. What this means is that these factors should be understood as experientially related, or associated in terms of their social context. Third, intervention should extend simultaneously in a variety of directions, instead of unfolding *ad seriatim*. This is because the realms of experience are not necessarily arranged sequentially or unidimensionally. And fourth, participation should be sought from every level of an organization, for the monopolization of information by any segment is unjustified. As should be noted, the continuous and direct integration supported by the systase is consistent with the social imagery that is essential to a culturally relevant intervention. Intervention is not a matter of systemic analysis, but instead involves identifying how relevant experiences are related and possibly influenced without disruption. In fine, the systase appears to be a necessary replacement for the system, in terms of supplying adequate imagery for supporting an organic or holistic program of intervention.

Decision-Making

The method whereby both practitioners and clients make decisions should be rethought. Typically persons are presumed to be "rational." Herbert Simon exemplifies this position when he remarks that rational persons are able to draw conclusions based on premises accepted by anyone who is normal.[32] Moreover, mentally competent individuals are assumed to utilize similar search strategies and classify input in an identical manner.

Consistent with dualism, reason is considered to be ahistorical. In other words, a reason is categorically removed from opinion. Whereas opinion is snarled in everyday concerns, reason is not. Reason is pristine and universal. Therefore, throughout the history of Western philosophy overcoming opinion has been viewed as prerequisite to discovering truth. How has this belief influenced the way in which decision-making has been conceived? According to Hubert and Stuart Dreyfus, four assumptions have been adopted. They refer to these as the biological, psychological, epistemological, and ontological assumptions.[33] And as a result of these presuppositions, decision-making is formalized.

The biological assumption relates to the belief that the mind consists of a network of off/on switches. A stimulus triggers a switch that causes the mind to act in an "all or none" manner. This assumption is refined further by the psychological premise that knowledge can be transformed into "bits" of information without any appreciable loss of meaning. Furthermore, according to the epistemological assumption, knowledge can be formalized without any distortion. Decision-making, accordingly, is described as following laws that are precise and uniform. So as not to contaminate this process, input must be quantified. As might be suspected, the key feature of the ontological assumption is that only quantifiable data lead to rational decision-making.

To insure that decision-making is understood to be rational, an abstract image of the mind has been introduced. Through formalizing the decision-making process, the illusion has been sustained that reason is anathema to opinion. Yet as recent research in the area of artificial intelligence illustrates, serious drawbacks accompany this version of reason. Restricted are the types of data, classificatory schemes, and logic that can be employed to reach conclusions. In this regard, both the input and output vital to the decision-making process are negatively affected.

Some modern writers reject this abstract conception of reason. They argue that reason should not be identified with merely classifying input correctly and following explicit rules of logic until clearly delineated conclusions are reached. But as long as this depiction of reason prevails, Terry Winograd notes correctly that decision-making will remain quite "brittle."[34] What he means is that reason will be disassociated from learning. Reason, stated otherwise, will remain separated from interpretation.

What Winograd is suggesting, along with Hubert and Stuart Dreyfus, is that the mind does not simply receive input, efficiently channel this information, and generate conclusions. In other words, the mind is not an "analytical engine."[35] Symbols are created by the mind, rather than simply uniformly processed. But when dualism is called in to question, the mind-world distinction cannot be maintained. Consequently, a creative bond exists between the mind and reality. Clearly this new image of the mind, and the resulting implications for decision-making, should be viewed as compatible with community-based intervention.

Undermining mind-world dualism requires that important facets of decision-making must be conceptualized anew. First, the mind should not be viewed as passive but as instrumental in evaluating information.

Second, facts should be understood to have a contingent character, which is a product of certain aims and commitments. And third, formal logic should not be thought to represent the most efficient way of connecting conclusions to premises. For presupposed by logic are social considerations about how reasoning should proceed. What all this means is that formalizing data collection and the manner in which knowledge is presented will not necessarily culminate in improved decision-making.

Yet the intent of formalizing key aspects of service delivery is to improve decision-making. The use of management information systems, standardized treatment plans, experimental evaluations, and computerized diagnostic schemes is supposed to result in the generation of reliable data, which can be used to make a manager's task more effective. Conceptual refinement and precise data are thought to lead to improved clinical and managerial judgments. In point of fact, most of the information management techniques that have been developed, such as the Delphi procedure, are devoted to resolving the logistical problems related to processing input. Moreover, the sudden popularity of management by objectives (MBO) among social service administrators, along with the use of client records based on the medical format, is believed to be consistent with the desire to facilitate rational decision-making. Pushed into the background, nonetheless, are the issues related to social relevance that are crucial for making culturally informed judgments.

Goal of Rehabilitation

Intervention is thought generally to result in the prevention or rehabilitation of disorders. The purpose of rehabilitation, however, is not at all clear. Broadly speaking, rehabilitation refers to the process whereby the health of a community or person is restored. Yet health is a nebulous state. Is health the absence of illness, or the condition of optimal well-being? And what considerations affect how these conditions are differentiated?

Typically an equilibrium model, couched in physiological terms, has been adopted to characterize the relationship between health and illness.[36] A system—natural or social—is assessed to be healthy as long as its equilibrium is maintained. Fluctuations around a norm should be expected, but these movements should not be very great. As a result, efficient equilibrations around a norm is evidence of a normally functioning system. Throughout this process a natural condition is assumed to exist which determines the range of fluctuations that can be tolerated without the system suffering any serious damage.

Yet when movement away from the norm occurs that is too great, danger is considered to be imminent. As noted by Parsons, for example, this situation must be corrected as soon as possible, or the well-being of the social system is thought to be in jeopardy.[37] In other words, little good results from periods of deviation. If nothing is done, in fact, the entire system can be thrown into serious disarray.

Intervention is supposed to prevent this crisis from happening. Plans should be implemented at the earliest opportunity, before fibrillation in the system can begin. Corrective action, however, usually consists of restoring a system to its natural condition. Moreover, this state is often associated with a set of conditions that should be met by any healthy system. For example, in a social system there is often assumed to exist "natural" rates of unemployment or inflation. Likewise, in a human system a natural level of stress is thought to be present. Hence deviance signals far more than a behavioral option, because the survival of the entire social or human system may be threatened by a significant departure from the norm.

Here again, dualism is manifested. Norms occupy an Archimedean point, while disequilibrium represents an absence of order. The point of intervention, accordingly, is to eliminate the causes of disorder and return harmony to the system, as a result of identifying and extinguishing certain behavior.

According to community-based practitioners, rehabilitation should not consist of adjusting clients to a norm that embodies a pre-established base-line. Instead, a community's code of decorum specifies a course for successful rehabilitation. Yet this does not mean that a community's social problems are necessarily normative. For example, a community may be ravaged by drug abuse, which is not viewed to be an acceptable habit. Drug use, on the contrary, may be the result of a community's inability to fulfill its aims. At this juncture, distinguishing normative from normal behavior may be helpful. Destructive coping behavior may be normative, for particular subsets of individuals, but is not normal by community standards.

From a community-based point of view, the aim of intervention should not be to restore equilibrium to a system. This rendition of rehabilitation is simply too abstract and, ultimately, unattainable. The goals and behavioral standards of a community, instead, should be facilitated through intervention. In this regard, norms that are self-imposed, rather than ideological, should serve as the reference point for determining disequilibrium. Equilibrium is thus transformed into an existential concept, so that the idea of harmony has social relevance.

Treatment Planning

Community-based practitioners should recognize that treatment planning is a multivalent activity. When formulating a client's treatment plan, in other words, a wide range of information should be consulted. Accordingly, a regimen of rehabilitation can be charted that is both socially responsive and comprehensive. Unfortunately this is not always the case, because the process of formulating and evaluating treatment plans is not very democratic.

Various mechanisms have been adopted to insure direct client involvement in the development of treatment plans.[38] For the most part, however, these changes have been superficial. For example, clients are supposed to be present at planning sessions and must sign their treatment plans. Input is solicited from clients, while they are given the opportunity to be fully informed about any course of action.

Nonetheless, the contribution that is made by clients to this process is usually negligible. They do not have at their disposal the information required to make knowledgeable statements. Indeed, who listens regularly to clients? This attitude is becoming increasingly prevalent, due to the increasing formalization and professionalization of service delivery. As a result of the introduction of more high-tech instruments, technical experts and their opinions are becoming more valuable. Hence clients are being moved further away from the center of the treatment process.

Often a treatment plan is described to be a contract that is enacted between a client and practitioner. Yet this portrayal is faulty, unless the asymmetrical relationship that exists between these persons is corrected. How can someone who is uninformed, in other words, enter rationally into a contract? Usually a contract is considered to be valid only when both parties are competent. But most often clients cannot meet this requirement. The information they need to make a wise decision is not widely disseminated, while their status as clients prohibits them from negotiating effectively with practitioners. As a result, during treatment planning sessions clients are simply made to feel that their desires are not rational.

At this juncture is where epistemological pluralism has obvious applicability. In addition to expanding the base of acceptable knowledge so that the views expressed by clients are not undermined by scientific themes or pseudotechnical rigor, the processes whereby treatment plans are discussed and implemented should be reexamined. Organizational barriers to knowledge acquisition and communication should be dismantled. This includes eliminating the status differentials that block access to or the appropriate consideration of information necessary to make culturally informed judgments. In other words, high-status experts should not be given the latitude to place certain knowledge "out of bounds." Implied by epistemological pluralism is that the application of knowledge should not be inhibited by organizational structures. For these imperatives can also be reassessed, because of their interpretive origin.

If input is desired from clients or the members of a community, the substantive changes required to encourage this participation will have to be made.[39] Moreover, the generation of information should be democratized. Coincident with the relativization of knowledge is the subversion of the center-periphery dualism. Consequently, according to Gebser, the "center is everywhere." All privileged positions are sacrificed, and input to the intervention process is unrestricted. And recommendations can be based on their merit, rather than their origin in an organization or supporters. Thus the openness required for true community-based treatment planning is possible.

Conclusion

Clearly, intervention does not occur in a vacuum. In fact, imagery guides how needs are assessed, data are collected, and treatment is undertaken. To call for the establishment of imagery consistent with the theory and practice of community-based intervention should not be viewed as terribly strange. Actually, promoting the conditions necessary for this type of intervention should have preceded the community mental health movement.

Nondualistic imagery, therefore, should inform the key stages of the intervention process. Central to this view is that everything occurs within the realm fragmented by dualism—that is, the *experience* that unites opposites. Accordingly, experience or human action should not be removed from intervention strategies. The "metaphysic" of intervention, in other words, must elevate in importance the human component that *defines* where normativeness and deviance begin. By focusing on this creative force, intervention can be socially attuned. In other words, community-based practitioners can be sensitized to the idea that every aspect of intervention should be value-based.

Notes

1. Rossi, Peter H., Howard E. Freeman, and Sonia R. Wright. *Evaluation A Systematic Approach.* (Beverly Hills, CA: Sage, 1979), pp. 18–51.
2. Habermas, Jürgen. *Legitimation Crisis.* (Boston: Beacon Press, 1975), pp. 10ff.

3. Husserl, Edmund. "Philosophy as Rigorous Science." In *Phenomenology and the Crisis of Philosophy*, by Edmund Husserl. (New York: Harper and Row, 1965), pp. 71–147.

4. Marcuse, Herbert. *Eros and Civilization*. (New York: Vintage Books, 1962), pp. 180–202.

5. Thompson, John B. *Studies in the Theory of Ideology*. (Berkeley: University of California Press, 1984), pp. 42–72.

6. Ibid., p. 45.

7. Schutz, Alfred. *Collected Papers, Vol. I.*. (The Hague: Nijhoff, 1962), p. 137.

8. Foucault, Michel. *Madness and Civilization*. (New York: Vintage, 1973), p. 86.

9. Pareto, Vilfredo. *The Mind and Society*. (New York: Harcourt, Brace, and Company, 1942), pp. 76–77.

10. Ibid., p. 88.

11. Binswanger, Ludwig. *Being-in-the-World*. (New York: Basic Books, 1963), pp. 149–181.

12. Felman, Shoshana. *Writing and Madness*. (Ithaca, NY: Cornell University Press, 1985), p. 19.

13. Hunt, Leon G. *Recent Spread of Heroin Use in the United States: Unanswered Questions*. (Washington, DC: Drug Abuse Council, 1974).

14. Schutz, *Collected Papers, Vol. I*, pp. 44–47.

15. Murphy, John W. and Joseph J. Pilotta. "Responsive Law and the Need for Community-Based Research," *Canadian Community Law Journal* 7, 1984, pp. 44–53.

16. Pilotta, Joseph, John W. Murphy, Tricia Jones, and Elizabeth Wilson. "Trends in Community Perception of Social Service Planning," *Evaluation and the Health Professions* 6(1), 1983, pp. 131–135.

17. Callaghan, Karen A., John W. Murphy, and Joseph J. Pilotta. "Technology and the Identification of Family Problems: Promises and Shortcomings," *Family Therapy* 13(1), 1986, pp. 95–104.

18. Butchvaron, Panayot. *Skepticism in Ethics*. (Bloomington, ID: Indiana University Press, 1989), pp. 47–48.

19. Murphy, John W., and John T. Pardeck. "The Computer-Micro-World, Knowledge, and Social Planning." In *Technology and Human Service Delivery*, ed. John W. Murphy and John T. Pardeck. (New York: The Haworth Press, 1988), pp. 127–141.

20. Dreyfus, Hubert L. *What Computers Can't Do*. (New York: Harper and Row, 1979).

21. Weber, Max. *The Methodology of the Social Sciences*. (Glencoe, IL: The Free Press, 1949), pp. 1–47.

22. Mannheim, Karl. "The Democratization of Culture." In *From Karl Mannheim*, ed. Kurt H. Wolff. (New York: Oxford University Press, 1971), pp. 271–346.

23. Deetz, Stanley A., and Edward L. McGlone. "An Interpretive Perspective on Testing and Measurement." In *Quantitative Methodology: Theory and Application*, ed. John W. Murphy and Joseph J. Pilotta. (Dubuque, IA: Kendall/Hunt, 1983), pp. 81–99.

24. Murphy, John W., John T. Pardeck, and Karen A. Callaghan. "The Ecological Model, Holism, and Socially Sensitive Counseling," *International Journal of Adolescence and Youth* 1(2), 1988, pp. 173–184.

25. von Bertalanffy, Ludwig. *Perspectives on General Systems Theory*. (New York: George Braziller, 1975), esp. pp. 40–52.

26. Ibid., pp. 149–169.

27. Murphy, John W. and Karen A. Callaghan. "System Theory and the Family: A Critique," *Early Child Development and Care* 39, 1988, pp. 163–176.

28. Sutherland, John W. *A General Systems Philosophy for the Social and Behavioral Sciences*. (New York: George Braziller, 1973), pp. 42–44.

29. Murphy, John W., "Organizational Issues in Worker Ownership," *The American Journal of Economics and Sociology*, 43(3), 1984, pp. 287–299.

30. Luhmann, Niklas. *The Differentiation of Society*. (New York: Columbia University Press, 1982), pp. 353–355.

31. Gebser, Jean. *The Ever-Present Origin*. (Athens, Ohio: Ohio University Press, 1985), pp. 309–310.

32. Simon, Herbert A. *Reasoning and Human Affairs*. (Oxford: Basil Blackwell, 1983), pp. 7–8.

33. Dreyfus, Hubert L. *What Computers Can't Do, pp. 155–227.*

34. Winograd, Terry. "A Procedure Model of Language Understanding." In *Computer Models of Thought and Language*, ed. Roger C. Schank and Kenneth Mark Colby. (San Francisco: W. H. Freeman Co., 1973), pp. 152–186.

35. Guattari, Felix. *Molecular Revolution*. (Middlesex, England: Penguin, 1984), pp. 135–143.

36. Gouldner, Alvin W. *The Coming Crisis of Western Sociology*. (New York: Basic Books, 1970), pp. 210–223.

37. Parson, Talcott. *The Social System*, pp. 297–321.

38. Kiresuk, Thomas J. and Sander H. Lund. "Process and Outcome Measurement Using Goal Attainment Scaling." In *Program Evaluation: Alcohol, Drug Abuse, and Mental Health Services*, ed. Jack Zusman and Cecil R. Wurster. (Lexington, MA: D.C. Health and Company, 1975), pp. 213–228.

39. Habermas, Jürgen. *Communication and the Evolution of Society*. (Boston: Beacon Press, 1979), pp. 1–68.

Chapter Six

Proyecto Bienestar: An Example of a Community-Based Intervention

Introduction

Throughout this volume the claim has been made that the original motives for the community mental health movement have been abandoned, and thus the focus of services has been increasingly restricted. Nevertheless, opportunities remain for innovative community-based programming, if these interventions can be shown to be technically feasible, financially viable, and clinically sound. Described in this chapter is an example of a community intervention that was undertaken in the Hispanic community. Such interventions provide an excellent proving ground for developing innovative strategies, which are truly grounded in the culture and social web-work of the local environment. Additionally, these interventions can provide community-based mental health practitioners with firmer programmatic guidelines than have been previously available, as well as empirical evidence of program efficacy that can bolster the case for expanded resources. Also, they constitute the finest context for training new practitioners and developing new knowledge.[1]

The focus of this chapter is an intervention designed for Hispanics, due to the familiarity of the authors with this experiment. Nonetheless, the community-based philosophy can be applied to any group, and this community-based intervention strategy can be replicated, after appropriate modification, in other ethnic minority populations. The approach described in this chapter is particularly well-suited for Mexican Americans, because these persons represent a rapidly increasing minority population in the United States. Furthermore, this group encompasses a large segment of individuals and families living below the poverty line. Therefore, they are a natural target group for public mental health services. But, as noted earlier, the customary behavior of Mexican Americans has been to stay away from such treatment. Novel intervention strategies are thus imperative, if this population is to be reached.

Low-income, minority communities are becoming increasingly disorganized, and adequate housing is rare. Gang activity, drug use, and teen pregnancy are chronic problems. Individuals at all stages in the life course are experiencing the effects of living in a deteriorating social environment. Existing mental health services are generally too fragmented and do not directly engage the community. Their focus is individuals who are malfunctioning to such a degree that these persons cannot be accommodated within family settings without extreme disruption. However, the seriously mentally ill do not constitute the largest class of individuals who require mental health services.[2] Rather, the most predominant category consists of those who are "at risk" for disabling mental health problems, or are already experiencing mild to moderate dysfunctions, primarily stemming from stressful environmental circumstances.

While accurately estimating the proportion of the minority population that could benefit from community-based interventions is difficult, a very cautious estimate can be surmised from the Epidemiologic Catchment Area Program sponsored by the NIMH. While the intention is not to reify research that has questionable cross-cultural validity for specific DSM-III disorders, these data may be useful as a broad gauge of community prevalence.[3] NIMH estimates are that 15.4 percent of respondents across five regional sites have experienced at least one disorder within the previous month.[4] An estimate limited to only low-income minority communities would clearly be higher. As a conservative figure, at any given time about 20 percent of minority community residents are probably experiencing distress and dysfunctions that result from mental health problems. An additional 10 percent could be considered "at risk" for such problems, although this figure will vary widely according to the sociodemographic and cultural characteristics of the minority group. Obviously, relying solely on clinical intervention is impractical, given the scope of the problem!

What We Do and Don't Know About Community Intervention

"What makes you think it will work?" This is often the first question asked by a clinician about the viability of a community-based intervention. Curiously, the question presupposes that clinically-based treatment has demonstrated efficacy, even though this is not the case for minority groups. In all candor, at this point, neither approach can produce a convincing track record. Based on evidence discussed below, however, community-based interventions are more adept at penetrating community networks and reaching a wider range of citizens than clinical interventions.

What remains to be done is to distinguish the types of people, problems, and settings that are most appropriate for clinical or community interventions. Parenthetically, these statements are not intended to set up a dichotomy. Rather, decisions about intervention feasibility should be based on careful community observation. Indeed, some minority communities may be so disorganized that community-based intervention is problematic. However, these types of communities are the exception. Certainly, in most low-income minority communities the social "vital signs" are still in place, thereby permitting community-based practitioners to have access to social networks and institutions for intervention purposes.

Some writers have said that, despite good intentions, the body of clinical knowledge, skills, and technology required to prevent mental disorders or psychological distress from occurring are not available.[5] And the same reservation could be stated about community-based remediation as well. The problem is further complicated by the cultural and regional diversity of minority populations, which makes problematic the notion that "standardized" interventions will have equal value in every situation. Nevertheless, much is known from the sociocultural and epidemiologic literature about the distribution of both various mental health problems and culturally related behaviors.[6] Furthermore, the influence of environmental factors is also better understood today than before, thus encouraging the cautious development of experimental interventions. To be sure, pioneering strategies should be concerned primarily with learning and environmental issues, and secondarily with the logistical problems related to program design and the pitfalls of day-to-day operations.

Based primarily on research pertaining to the sociopsychological aspects of stress, a body of theory has emerged to guide the formulation of interventions that can be used to prevent or disrupt the formation of mental health problems.[7] As noted by Roskin, the common components of these intervention models include the following: (a) modification of the environment as it distresses and supports; (b) provision of opportunities for strengthening individual capacities for dealing with interpersonal relationships; (c) understanding and coping with anticipated critical development tasks; and, (d) understanding and coping with unanticipated stressful life situations.[8] These broad guidelines can be tailored according to the nature of the community, the target individuals, and the type of problem that is addressed. In some instances, environmental factors may be paramount, while in others the development of specific social skills or coping abilities may be most important. In any case, the aim of these intervention strategies is to empower individuals and groups to modify their environments.

Accessing Target Populations

For traditional practitioners, accessing minority communities may be the most serious challenge in launching community-based interventions. Since CMHCs are almost totally committed to clinical services, the logic of community entry and the "how to" of engaging natural networks and community institutions is seldom part of the repertoire of knowledge possessed by practitioners.[9] If a target group is identified by some method, for example, by the use of epidemiological surveys, rates-in-treatment information, or projection models, how can this target group be better understood or entered at the community level for intervention purposes?

If an intervention is to be community-based, information should be obtained about life-styles and behavioral patterns of community residents, especially about those who fall into the "at-risk" category suitable for intervention. There are multiple sources for this information, and most experienced practitioners have acquired much of this data, systematically or otherwise, from clinical experience with minority group members. However, there are specific methods that can be used to gather additional information and provide community access that are simple to employ, and can supply a continuous stream of information about changing conditions in a community and its informal interactional patterns.

The cultural foundation of the intervention described in this chapter is based on the work of Valle and his colleagues, which describes how social networks function in the Mexican American community.[10] In particular, this body of research identifies various classes of natural networks, as well as the characteristics of their members. Hence, several types of natural helpers are described that have implications for community-based interventions. In brief, natural helpers can be distinguished by the role they play in a community and the kinds of interaction in which they are involved. To concretize this statement, the natural helpers that are most likely to be found in "grassroots" social networks typically address the everyday problems of neighbors, friends, and acquaintances found within their spatial or cultural environment.

Practitioners who wish to gain access to these networks should be aware of several key signs. Reciprocity networks in the context of Mexican American culture presuppose establishing intimate social ties, or *con-*

fianza, that are validated through appropriate oral and behavioral transactions.[11] Therefore, the content and style of these transactions should be well understood by the practitioner. The resulting *confianza* network becomes an enduring resource for its members, which transcends the limitations of formal kinship patterns. Natural helpers who operate within this type of primary group are concerned with giving instrumental and emotional support to other individuals who are fundamentally similar to them in numerous ways, in a setting that is characterized by a scarcity of resources. This is an orientation that is different from that exhibited by a middle-level community agency employee, who is a professional broker of services. However, there may be some overlap between these orientations, especially in multiservice agencies where paraprofessionals or volunteers are employed to deal with community residents. Practitioners need to be aware of these variations when they attempt to intervene with informal networks.

A specific variant of the *confianza* network has been designated by Valle and Bensussen as the "linkperson" structure. Members of such a network are linked through specialized roles. There is a significant amount of literature that describes how these roles are related to health, counseling, and spiritual needs.[12] For example, *curanderos* (healers), *sobadores* (masseuses), *yerberos* (herbalists), *hueseros* (lay chiropractors), and *espiritualistas* (spiritualists) are specialists whose services can be acquired by being linked to the appropriate network.[13] If persons are not members of the "linkperson" network, but are seeking services from a special provider, they can enter this constellation as a result of a personal introduction or, in some instances, by word-of-mouth.

However, linkperson networks usually contain many more individuals with a less well-defined service function, but who are equally committed to playing an instrumental role for other participants. These individuals vary both in terms of what they can offer and in their level of sophistication. For example, in a low-income neighborhood there may be a neighbor who is home during the day and has a car, knows how to drive it, and is disposed to helping people on his or her block with their problems, which may include finding transportation to the doctor's office or to the store. In another instance, someone may also have highly developed social skills, including perhaps bilingual fluency and the ability to negotiate recurring problems with school officials, insurance adjusters, or government bureaucrats that are often enigmatic to ethnic-minority people who have not yet mastered the English language. In return for these services, those who have been helped respond by providing other services or goods, although the resulting reciprocity does not have to be completely symmetrical.

Preceding the intervention described below, a list of criteria that describe the indigenous network helper was formulated, and personnel in local churches, human services agencies, schools, stores, and neighborhood level voluntary organizations were approached and asked to nominate candidates. When a core of these helpers was found, they were screened in order to verify whether they possessed the requisite characteristics. This pool of residents helped, in turn, to identify others like themselves. For obvious reasons, these natural helpers provide very valuable information about how microsocial networks function and facilitate community entry by getting information into these networks.[14] This approach is automatically community-grounded, because these helpers provide a rich source of ethnographic information and can assist with staff training, or reviewing and refining intervention and assessment materials that are to be used with the target population. Natural network helpers do not have to function as interviewers, although this was the intent in the intervention that is described below.

Clearly this example is pertinent to Hispanics. But parallel helpers can be found in all ethnic minority populations, although their characteristics and *modus operandi* may differ significantly from group to group.[15] More often than not, these caregivers are pleased to participate in the formulation of interventions and feel complimented by the recognition that they receive.

In community intervention, given the setting, practitioners should not expect to exercise the same amount of control that is possible in a clinical environment. Therefore, formal "client" screening should be exchanged for other tactics that will assist in identifying individuals who are appropriate to facilitate interventions. Cultural etiquette in minority communities may not allow for the simple partitioning of individuals based on levels of dysfunction or some other preordained clinical criteria, and thus a great deal of internal variance should be accommodated. This can actually work to the benefit of interventions during the recruitment phase. For example, if an intervention calls for group sessions at the homes of participants, some individuals may choose to bring friends who they think will enjoy these events. This process is similar to the "snowball" sampling technique used by anthropologists with *sub rosa* populations.[16] Each contact branches to new contacts, until the informal network of eligibles is exhausted.

Because of the "snowball" effect, community interventions are likely to act as a networking and *triage* service. The "early adopters" of the intervention, to use Rodgers term, will disseminate information about the program, thereby producing a powerful secondary recruitment method.[17]

As this process unfolds, a wide range of needs may be uncovered while people are funneled toward services. As noted above, one result is that individuals who are outside of the original target group may also "get into the network." Many of these nontarget clients may be candidates for unique types of interventions and services. As most community practitioners realize, personal problems usually come in clusters and require diverse resources for amelioration. Identifying networks may assist in illustrating the context of problems, along with the social patterns of maladies.

Theoretical Justification for Intervention

Community intervention also presupposes that practitioners have formulated a coherent and culturally grounded "theory of the problem," which is really an orienting statement rather than an intervention theory or model. The purpose of this descriptive thesis is to provide a contextual understanding regarding how psychosocial factors and processes contribute to the problem in question.[18] However, this cannot be done without amassing information derived from multiple sources. Often the results of dedicated surveys and ethnographic studies are available, and when combined with other sources of data, such as the case reports of social workers, a body of sensitive knowledge is produced to guide an intervention project. An example of establishing a "theory of the problem" is provided by the *Proyecto Bienestar* intervention.

The use of social learning theory in community intervention is very common today, and was integral to this study.[19] While this theory is potentially useful for this purpose, there are dangers in simply transferring conceptual models into different social or cultural domains. For example, social learning theory has not really been evaluated for use in differing cultural contexts. Therefore, no one knows whether key mechanisms such as "self-efficacy" have equivalent meaning across cultures. Basic research regarding the role of culture in cognitive functioning is needed. Conceivably, within self-effacing cultures, the concept of "self-efficacy" would be difficult to define or propose as a basis for cognitive restructuring or behavioral change.

Case Study of Proyecto Bienestar

It is almost a truism that you only learn how to conduct a community intervention properly by undertaking one. Nevertheless, much can be learned by reviewing the experience of others. To this end, a particular intervention conducted in California is presented in order to illustrate the process whereby a community-based intervention is conceptualized, organized, and evaluated. The content and design of this intervention should not necessarily be transferred *in toto* to other interventions, although the stages of development are probably generalizable. The intervention was intended for low-income women of Mexican descent; the target problem was depression. In this instance, the intervention assumed the form of a randomized trial within a community, with strict design procedures and outcome measures. Although the intent is to present only a summary, sufficient information is provided to permit adequate comprehension of how this project was operationalized and evaluated. Readers who desire greater technical information are encouraged to consult Vega et al.[20]

Target Population

The selection of the target group for intervention was based on a multifaceted assessment procedure. A series of California epidemiologic studies were reviewed in order to identify the subgroups at risk for psychological distress in the Mexican American population.[21] The greatest risk was associated with being in mid-life, having a low income, recently becoming an immigrant, and being a female. Several other bases of information were tapped as well. These included clinical impressions of practitioners, ethnographic observations, and formal research about gender roles, family structure, and normative patterns in this cohort of women.

When entering middle age (approximately forty years of age), low-income Mexican American women are faced with changing role expectations. They have been dependent on their husbands for income and for the management of many external obligations. If they are immigrants, they often have minimal English language skills, and their social competence for manipulating the environment outside of their homes is limited. Their husbands, who have labored most often in occupations that are physically demanding, are usually reaching a point of declining productivity. In fact, working-class Mexican American males, despite having a very low rate of health problems as young adults, are prone to physical disability in middle age and beyond. Since this type of employment offers little reward when a worker's physical competence begins to decline, occupational instability and a corresponding decline in earning power often occur. When this situation comes to pass, the entire family must adjust, especially the wife who faces an uncertain future and changing role demands. Some of the time, she may have to become more active in generating income, as well as in managing the external affairs of the family. Obviously, these women are thrown into a very difficult situation, which places them under chronic stress. Their psychological and emotional resilience is thus often seriously impaired.

Another key finding from sociocultural research is that immigrants tend to have smaller social networks than native-born Mexican Americans or non-Hispanic whites, and the social networks of immigrants are more likely to be comprised of family members.[22] Although these networks appear to be fairly stable, there exists a significant percentage of women within this group who report limited network contact or social support. Another burden relates to the absence of supportive interactions within these frameworks. Although the stereotype of Mexican Americans usually brings to mind the notion of a large and enmeshed family structure, in reality there are wide variations in living arrangements as well as cohesiveness within these families.[23] Further, a significant percentage of female-headed households can also be found.

Since women in this cohort commence child rearing at relatively young ages and have a long period of childbearing thereafter, young adults often start independent households when their mothers are not yet forty years of age and still have young children in the home. This creates a situation somewhat different from the classic "extended" family, in that these new families are not living under the same roof, but tend to reside nearby and remain in close contact with the parental households. Furthermore, this pattern tends to be more typical of daughters than of sons, because the former are more likely to interact frequently with their mothers. However, although the interaction levels are high in these situations, this relationship is often more supportive for the adult children than for the mothers, who are extending a great deal of instrumental and emotional support to their children. This support comes in the form of material assistance, child care, and affective nurturance, when their children are experiencing serious life-change problems related to poverty, unemployment, and marital conflicts. This maternal support is expected, whether or not the Mexican American mother is really in a position to provide this resource.

Therefore, these women are entering a life stage where there is an increasing risk for psychological distress. Also, these risk factors are mutually reinforcing. Economic marginality sustains a situation of protracted life strain and increases the possibility of negative life changes. Furthermore, this process creates the social context for role overload and the negative psychological effects of decreasing marital satisfaction. In short, this is the "theory of the problem" that underlies the intervention. The solution is to create a sense of "empowerment" among these women, so that their problems appear to be manageable, and to provide a model for acquiring specific skills that will increase their ability to manipulate their environment. Although this information does not spell out in detail the best way to intervene successfully with these women, the problem is certainly concretized.

Theoretical Basis of the Research

In order to intervene effectively with this cohort, there should be a conceptual blueprint to guide the content of intervention and the implementation strategy. In this case, the necessary conceptual orientation emerged from two distinct domains that were synthesized. The first was social learning theory, which was used to create a "cognitive-behavioral educational" program. The goal of this program was to prevent the onset of depressive symptoms by increasing the coping ability of "at risk" women. These persons were taught how to reorganize their environment, so that ultimately various sources of stress could be reduced or eliminated altogether. Social learning theory holds that the best predictor of future behavior is past actions, unless something modifies this situation. Typically, new behavior can be introduced by modeling, behavioral rehearsal, and continued social reinforcement. Moderate increases in task complexity, associated with learning new behaviors, is linked to a growing awareness of increasing personal competence.[24]

According to social learning theory, the cognitive mechanism that is related to exhibiting new behaviors is called "self-efficacy." Logically, the first step is to increase a person's confidence level by providing information, cognitive skills, and environmental support. Increasing levels of self-efficacy are reinforced by actual task mastery, because cognition and behavioral reinforcement are inherently related. In *Proyecto Bienestar* this process had three major phases. First, *confianza* was established through culturally sanctioned methods, which was the *forte* of the *servidoras* (culturally based helpers found within the Mexican American community). Then participants were encouraged to think about their past experiences, especially about difficult circumstances in their past that they had surmounted and which demonstrated their individual as well as cultural strengths. Second, techniques of self-assertion were taught, including tactics for accessing information and resources and negotiating with various types of agency or institutional personnel. Third, cognitive coping skills, such as learning how to divide complex situations into manageable units, were emphasized. In addition, participants were taught how to distinguish effective cognitive coping responses from those that only serve to frustrate the identification of solutions to a problem.

These three foci were emphasized by using multiple approaches, including written information, graphic illustrations, and oral presentations. The logic of the curriculum was to present the major themes of the intervention and reinforce them through social learning process, as a result of using diverse strategies and materials. However, materials were not introduced in a rigid manner, because people move at quite different speed through the learning process. Similarly, the content of the curriculum was flexible, for at the beginning of the intervention an accurate determination could not be made about which materials would be effective. In other words, the theoretical guideposts and foci of the intervention were clearly established, but the actual implementation was developmental and guided by actual field experience.

However, the use of social learning theory has certain pitfalls. In general, the conceptual ancestry of this theory is not necessarily conducive to social sensitivity. After all, behaviorism has severe limitations. First, if people are given tasks that they are not ready to handle, and they fail in their efforts, there can be a serious deterioration in task mastery, and thus negative attitudes may develop about the goals and methods of an intervention. Also, since behavioral change is highly unstable, and regression to old behaviors is likely, people must be taught to deal with the sense of anxiety, futility, or hopelessness that this reversal may engender. Second, social learning theory is not necessarily culturally grounded. Although useful as a general orienting model, social learning theory does not provide formulae for creating culturally sensitive intervention tactics, educational materials, and evaluation criteria. Third, even though having complete information before commencing intervention activities is desirable, all interventions are learn-as-you-go ventures. The process of intervention reveals more about the strengths and weaknesses of a particular approach than anything else, and provides a dynamic source of feedback to practitioners for refining interventions *in vivo*.

Thus social learning theory was modified throughout this project, so that this viewpoint remained compatible with the community's world view. In this example, ethnographic observation helped to provide information that was useful for designing an intervention according to the social learning model. The rich foundation of reciprocity behaviors that exists in Mexican American culture provided a tangible basis for accessing the target population. Moreover, the mutually supportive behavior found in this Hispanic community was consonant with the assumptions of social learning theory.

Of importance to practitioners should be the fact that there are culturally correct ways for getting into a target group, and most likely precedents have been established for gaining access to the necessary social networks. The Mexican American community is no exception, as indicated in the previous discussion about natural helpers. In this instance, the spanish word *servidora* is used in the feminine gender only as an illustration, since individuals of either sex can occupy this role. As pointed out by Valle and others, the characteristics of these helpers and their role specialization are a consequence of both personal attributes and their participation in particular social networks. For example, the type of natural helper required for this intervention functions primarily within the *confianza* social networks, thereby stressing primary group behaviors such as service and resource distribution rather than secondary group activities that are formal, task-oriented, and based on the exercise of power. This is an important distinction that is worthy of reiteration.

Since the *servidoras* are socially and culturally similar to the target group, they supply role models that are also consistent with the requirements of learning theory. Additionally, these persons exhibit the types of self-efficacy that this intervention sought to promote. Helpers have faced similar living conditions as clients and have developed a repertoire of personal skills for solving problems. However, this is not the same as saying that *servidoras* are qualified to teach these skills in a way that is consistent with the logic of social learning theory. This is why these individuals were carefully screened, and that a structured curriculum was developed in concert with them. Moreover, *servidora* training included a review of all intervention materials and regular debriefings to assess their strengths and weaknesses, along with discussing any confusion that might be associated with implementing various intervention tactics. An interesting by-product of this training-monitoring process was the powerful bonding effect that took place among the *servidoras*, so that years after the termination of intervention activities they continued to meet on their own to discuss issues of common interest, including the progress of the women they helped or still continue to contact.

Design of the Intervention

This intervention used a classic experimental design consisting of four stages. First, a community population was screened in order to identify eligible "risk-group" members on the basis of ethnicity, age (between thirty-five and fifty), and socioeconomic status. Screening was undertaken by women who were from the same types of communities where they conducted interviews. However, they were not allowed to interview people they knew personally. Nor were interviewers allowed to become *servidora* interveners. Screening was done on a door-to-door basis, in neighborhoods with moderate to high proportions of Mexican Americans. At the time of this screening, a short depression checklist was used to identify and eliminate those who had high levels of current depressive symptoms, since the project was designed as an early preventive intervention for women who are either entering into or are already within the age range of enhanced risk for depression.

Since virtually all of the participants in this intervention were native Spanish speakers, the issue of cultural and linguistic equivalence was paramount. All measures, including the depression checklist, were reviewed by the *servidoras*, as a way to establish the face validity of the measures and content equivalence from English versions.[25] Standard translation and back-translation procedures that employed independent community judges were also used, and differences of opinion were resolved in conferences that included project staff members who were bilingual. Finally the depression measure was pilot tested in the community and proved to be very satisfactory.

The second stage of screening involved administering a comprehensive base-line interview. This included an assessment of serious health or psychiatric impairments. Individuals suffering from these problems were also removed from the intervention for the same reasons mentioned previously. The point should be made at this juncture that if this intervention had not been conducted as a strict community trial, this extensive screening would have been unnecessary. Nevertheless, rigorous screening provided a relatively homogeneous sample appropriate for the nature of this intervention.

The third stage of the process involved the randomization of the 655 remaining eligibles into three conditions, including one control and two intervention groups. While the educational content for both intervention groups was similar, one intervention stressed one-to-one contact between *servidoras* and eligible women in their homes, while the second intervention was based on group sessions held in community settings. The one-to-one approach was called the "linkperson" strategy, and most closely approximated the naturally occurring network interactions and reciprocity behavior found in Mexican American culture. The group approach was called the *merienda* intervention, because within Mexican culture this word connotes the sharing of light refreshments in a congenial atmosphere.

Servidoras were trained separately for each intervention modality, and none were allowed to conduct both types of interventions. *Merienda servidoras* used a wider assortment of techniques derived from social learning theory, especially related to the collective reinforcement of behavioral goals. On the other hand, the "linkperson" modality was more in keeping with regular social network dynamics and, as indicative of this mode of interaction, did not require women to leave their homes. Since many of these women were literally "embedded" within family obligations, many of them had little experience in venturing out to engage in activity that was exclusively intended for their use or pleasure.

Remarkably, about one half of the women who were randomized into intervention groups actually participated in at least one session. To put this statement in perspective, readers should recall that the women were randomized first, and then asked to participate in sessions. This was a true community population that was approached "cold" and, further, had no reason to believe that they were at any risk of having psychological problems. A careful analysis of participation revealed that self-selection did take place, in that those with higher levels of depressive symptoms were more likely to show up and participate in a greater number of intervention sessions. The *merienda* intervention was conducted over a period of approximately twelve weeks, with one session held each week. The "linkperson" contacts lasted about twelve weeks as well. Retrospectively, the intervention period should have been longer. Indeed, some participants continued to meet even without the benefit of having any formal direction from the *servidoras*. The final component of the design was the outcome assessment.

Outcome Assessment

Six months after the termination of intervention activities an outcome measure was used to determine the effectiveness of the program. Approximately three-quarters of the original randomized eligibles were reinterviewed. Outcome was defined primarily as the difference in mean scores on depression between the baseline and the post-intervention measure. The intervention results are complex and can be interpreted in a number of ways. However, at this time the most strict interpretation required by the use of an experimental design will be offered, which requires a comparison of experimental and control groups. In a very real sense, this "loads" the results in the direction of not showing intervention effects, because half of the eligibles, though assigned to intervention groups, actually never participated. Therefore, the effects of the intervention must be strong enough among participants to "carry" the other half, who never had anything to do with the intervention but were still considered to be members of the intervention group.

The results can be summarized as follows: (1) a comparison of the intervention groups against the control group indicates no statistically significant differences; (2) an outcome comparison of only intervention subjects who were asymptomatic or had very low symptoms at baseline with similar controls indicates a statistically significant prevention effect for both intervention modalities; (3) those who actively participated in interventions are more likely to have reduced symptom levels than those who refused participation or dropped out early; and (4) intervention effects are similar for both intervention modalities. Overall, the intervention appears to work among those women who were the true target for this intervention, in other words, those who are asymptomatic or minimally symptomatic. This program worked less well among those who already had moderate levels of symptoms and dysfunctions.

In case the reader is wondering how people with moderate symptoms at baseline entered the eligible pool despite the extensive screening, this point will be clarified. The second screening took place several months after the first, and the former involved a screening that used a diagnostic protocol only.[26] Therefore, some women who had moderate symptoms, but did not meet the criteria for a formal diagnosis, did enter the sample. Clearly, if the eligible pool had been limited to asymptomatic or low symptomatic women who elected to participate, the effects would have been much stronger than the comparison shows. On the other hand, the experience of including a range of symptoms levels is instructive, because one additional finding is that this intervention is not effective as a treatment method among women who are significantly depressed.

Implications of Proyecto Bienestar

No one is suggesting or implying that this type of intervention should constitute a standard for the field. Rather, this intervention is briefly described only to illustrate one approach that is suitable for a specific cultural group. Furthermore, this approach illustrates a particular class of interventions that is aimed at individuals. Other types of interventions may be targeted differently. For example, reducing alcohol abuse may be easier by curtailing the sale of alcohol products than by convincing people to change their drinking behavior. Similarly, in the mental health arena, better housing conditions and improved employment opportunities may improve mental health in a more direct fashion than by using person-centered interventions. Other more broad-based interventions may be mass media oriented, or linked to local health providers who can reach a large number of people.

The point is that there are many things that can be done to improve the mental health status of minority populations, and most of these strategies are not mutually exclusive. Clearly, a gradient of different classes and types of interventions can be created, as a result of identifying multiple sites and domains of life for instituting these practices. Already Munoz has discussed a range of access points, intervention materials, and technologies that are suitable for mental health prevention efforts intended for Hispanic cultural groups.[27] Elsewhere, the *merienda* approach described above has been reformulated in order to create the core of a cardiovascular risk-reduction project, entitled "*Por La Vida*." This fusion of approaches included using the *merienda* modality and various techniques that promoted relaxation and self-efficacy.

The strategy described in this chapter is a feasible community-based intervention that could be implemented by a local agency, such as a CMHC. However, there are significant issues related to the management and implementation of this intervention that should be discussed, in order to illustrate some of the problems that are faced generally when conducting a community intervention. Whether the interveners are professional practitioners or community residents, they must be carefully selected, trained, and monitored. In an educational intervention, the interveners must be convinced of the value of the intervention, as well as their capability to impart it successfully, or the project will not be successful. Another concern relates to intervenor "burnout," especially when the intervention is labor-intensive or the target group is saturated with serious personal problems. Interveners should be rotated under these conditions, or given periodic nonintervention assignments.

Poorly managed interventions may do more harm than good, as a result of turning a community against a project. As with community-based interventions in general, in *Proyecto Bienestar* special attention was given to insure the proper use of idiomatic expressions and cultural imagery. Furthermore, care was taken to avoid the inadvertent use of stereotypes and negative messages. Evidence was gathered to ascertain whether the educational message was being received and understood in the manner intended by the intervenor. Additionally, printed media were attractive, relevant, and self-explanatory. Images intended to portray members of a cultural group were field tested, so that they were not offensive and reflected current self-perceptions. All the practitioners understood that when intervening with Hispanics there is no such thing as "standard" Spanish. Accommodating the local linguistic style was recognized to be essential. Therefore, everything should be checked out with community residents in advance, and "off-the-shelf" materials developed for use with a particular group should be adopted only with caution.

Hispanics are very sensitive about mental health problems and the meaning of psychological dysfunctions. There can be tremendous potential for embarrassment, shame, and denial related to this issue.[28] This is particularly true if a cultural group tends to view mental illness as a sign of personal failure, biological inferiority, or an incurable disease. Indeed, the first stage of a community-based intervention should be to inform communities about the range of definitions that pertain to mental health and mental illness. The dominant medical presuppositions should be illustrated as limited, so that community members are not embarrassed or intimidated to discuss their actual experiences. For example, phenomenologists describe this process by using the phrase *zur Sache selbst*, or "getting back to the things themselves."[29] Their point is that experiences should be recorded and understood before they are reinterpreted by medical protocol, in order to obtain undistorted knowledge.

Every effort should be made to combine interventions with various methods of collecting information about those who are directly contacted, as well as the community at large. The utility of information about a community quickly decreases with time, as social conditions, residential patterns, and migration change. Therefore, a simple but reliable method of collecting useful information on an ongoing basis is preferable to "super" studies. Knowing how to use the information most effectively is a product of experience and collaborative effort. Accordingly, at least initially, the know-how of university researchers and community-based practitioners should be merged.

Many people who plan behavioral interventions with ethnic minorities commonly overlook three important things. First, methods of accessing the target group are often not culturally-grounded. Therefore, they take little heed of the daily life-style patterns of minorities, which would provide a realistic appraisal of the potential for capturing the members of the target group within a specific domain, for example, a school, workplace, recreation or community center, church, and so on. Second, educational interventions do not necessarily increase in effectiveness past a certain point of exposure, so there is a danger of being too linear and inadvertently overlooking a community's sense of time and level of interest.[30] Third, community interventions rarely last long enough to create enduring behavior change. In part, this is an artifact of financial support and staffing availability. Nonetheless, this point should not be confused with the previous one. The idea is to make interventions more fluid, so that they have a natural fit within the context of minority life styles and communities.

Conclusion

The goal of this chapter is to introduce readers to how community-based interventions can be formulated, and to present a case study of an experimental intervention. Undoubtedly, more questions are raised than are answered. There are no standard interventions, because every practitioner faces a unique set of circumstances. Nevertheless, some basic strategies and pitfalls derived from an actual field trial are brought to light. Underscored here is the importance of using a theoretical scheme for organizing all phases of an intervention that does not obscure the community.

Increasingly, practitioners are coming to realize that there is a fundamental distinction between technical and communicative competence. The former refers to the standard set of capabilities that are learned derived from traditional methodological exercises. On the other hand, the latter pertains to the ability to interact on a daily basis with community residents, and this skill is only acquired through reflexive or self-critical involvement in cultural enclaves, environmental settings, and interpersonal networks. Clearly both types of competence are required for successful community intervention.

The synthesis of technological and communicative competence can yield new methodologies that are useful for revising the manner in which minority communities are understood. These methodologies rely heavily on tapping interactional networks and identifying "key citizens" for information. They also require that cultural information be "played back" to the people who reside within minority communities, before data becomes fact. Every phase of a community-based intervention, in other words, should incorporate reflexivity from conceptualization through the interpretation of results. *Proyecto Bienestar* is simply an illustration of one way to undertake this sort of endeavor.

Notes

1. Cowen, Emory L., "The Wooing of Primary Prevention," *American Journal of Community Psychology* 8(3), 1980, pp. 258–284.

2. Link, Bruce and Bruce Dohrenwend. "Formulation of Hypotheses About the True Prevalence of Demoralization in the United States." In *Mental Illness in the United States*, ed. Bruce Dohrenwend, et al. (New York: Praeger, 1980).

3. Robins, Lee N. "Cross-Cultural Differences in Psychiatric Disorder," *American Journal of Public Health* 79(11), 1989, pp. 1479–1480.

4. Regier, Darrel A., Jeffrey H. Boyd, Jack D. Burke, et al. "One Month Prevalence of Mental Disorder in the United States," *Archives of General Psychiatry* 45(11), 1988, pp. 977–986.

5. Lamb, H. Richard, Jack Zusman. "Primary Prevention in Perspective," *American Journal of Psychiatry* 136(1), 1979, pp. 12–17.

6. Mezzich, Juan E. and Carlos E. Berganzo (eds.). *Culture and Psychopathology*. (New York: Columbia University Press, 1984).

7. Lazarus, Richard and Susan Folkman. *Stress, Appraisal and Coping*. (New York: Springer, 1984).

8. Roskin, Michael. "Coping With Life Changes—A Preventive Social Work Approach," *American Journal of Community Psychology* 10(3), 1982, pp. 331–340.

9. Valle, Ramon. "A Natural Resource System for Health-Mental Health Promotions to Latino/Hispanic Populations." In *Hispanic Natural Support System*, ed. William Vega and Ramon Valle. (Sacramento, CA: Department of Mental Health, 1982), pp. 35–44.

10. Valle, Ramon and Lydia Mendoza. *The Elder Latino*. (San Diego, CA: Campanile Press, 1978); Valle, Ramon. "Hispanic Social Networks and Prevention." In *Psychiatric Epidemiology and Prevention: The Possibilities*, ed. Richard L. Hough, Patricia A. Gongolo, Vivian B. Brown and Stephen E. Goldston. (Los Angeles: University of California Neuropsychiatric Institute, 1985), pp. 131–157; Valle, Ramon and Carlos Martinez. "Natural Networks of Elderly Hispanics of Mexican Heritage: Implications for Mental Health." In *Chicano Aging and Mental Health*, ed. M. Miranda and Raul A. Ruiz. (Rockville, MD: DHHS Pub. No. (ADM) 81–952, 1981), pp. 76–117.

11. Velez-Ibanez, Carlos. *Rituals of Marginality*. (Berkeley: University of California Press, 1983).

12. Valle, Ramon and Gloria Bensussen. "Hispanic Social Networks, Social Support and Mental Health." In *Stress and Hispanic Mental Health*, ed. William A. Vega and Manuel R. Miranda. (Rockville, MD: DHHS Pub. No. (ADM) 85–1410, 1985), pp. 147–173.

13. Mendoza, Lydia. *The Servidor System: Policy Implications for Elderly Hispanics*. (San Diego, CA: Center on Aging, San Diego State University, 1981).

14. Valle, Ramon. "Social Mapping Techniques." In *Hispanic Natural Support Network*, ed. William A. Vega and Manuel R. Miranda. (Sacramento, CA: Department of Mental Health, 1982), pp. 113–121.

15. Vallance, Theodore R. and Anthony R. D'Aygelli. "The Helping Community: Characteristics of Natural Helpers," *American Journal of Community Psychology* 10(2), 1982, pp. 197–205.

16. Chavez, Leo. "Settlers and Sojourners: The Core of Mexicans in the United States," *Human Organization* 47(2), 1988, pp. 95–108.

17. Rodgers, E. M. *The Diffusion of Innovation, Third Edition*. (New York: The Free Press, 1983).

18. Price, Richard. *Priorities for Prevention Research: Linking Risk Factors and Intervention Research*. Unpublished paper. (Ann Arbor, MI: University of Michigan, 1981).

19. Bandura, Albert. "Self-Efficacy: Toward a Unifying Theory of Behavioral Change," *Psychological Bulletin* 84(2), 1977, pp. 191–215.

20. Vega, William, Ramon Valle, Bakdon Kolody, and Richard Hough. "The Hispanic Network Preventive Intervention Study." In *The Prevention of Depression: Research Foundations*, ed. R. Manoz. (New York: Hemisphere, 1987), pp. 217–234.

21. Vega, William A., George J. Warheit, and Kenneth Meinhardt. "Mental Health Issues in the Hispanic Community: The Prevalence of Psychological Distress." In *Stress and Hispanic Mental Health*, ed. William A. Vega and Manuel R. Miranda. (Rochester, MD: DHHS Pub. No. (ADM) 85–1410, 1985), pp. 30–47.

22. Keefe, Susan. "Real and Ideal Familism Among Mexican Americans and Anglo Americans: On the Meaning of 'Close' Family Ties," *Human Organization* 43(1), 1984, pp. 65–70.

23. Sena-Riviera, Jaime. "Extended Kinship in the United States: Competing Models and the Case of La Familia Chicana," *Journal of Marriage and the Family* 41(1), 1979, pp. 121–139.

24. Bandura, Albert. *Social Learning Theory*. (Englewood Cliffs, NJ: Prentice-Hall, 1977).

25. Radloff, Lenore. "The CES-D Scale: A Self Report Depression Scale for Research in the General Population," *Applied Psychological Measurement* 1(2), 1977, 385–401.

26. Robins, Lee, John Helzer, Jack Croughon, and Kathryn Ratcliff. "The NIMH Diagnostic Interview Schedule: Its History, Characteristics, and Validity," *Archives of General Psychiatry* 38(4), 1981, pp. 381–389.

27. Munoz, Ricardo F. "A Strategy for the Prevention of Psychological Problems in Latinos: Employing Accessibility and Effectiveness." In *Hispanic Natural Support Systems*, ed. William Vega and Ramon Valle. (Sacramento, CA: Mental Health Department, 1982), pp. 85–96.

28. Karno, Marvin, and Robert B. Edgerton. "Perception of Mental Illness in a Mexican American Community," *Archives of General Psychiatry* 20(2), 1969, pp. 233–238.

29. Husserl, Edmund. *The Idea of Phenomenology*. (The Hague: Nijhoff, 1964).

30. Vega, William, James Sallis, Thomas Patterson, et al. "Predictors of Dietary Change in Mexican American Families Participating in a Health Behavior Change Program," *American Journal of Preventive Medicine* 4(4), 1988, pp. 194–199.

Chapter Seven

Programmatic Changes and Citizen Involvement

Introduction

The aim of this volume has been to outline, in theoretical terms, the potential nondualistic character of community-based intervention. At this juncture, some practical implications of a very broad philosophical position will be addressed. In other words, what policy or programmatic changes should be implemented subsequent to accepting the theoretical premises of this approach to intervention? As might be suspected, many of these practical considerations relate closely to the philosophical issues that have been raised.

Anyone who attempts to develop a guide to community-based or culturally sensitive intervention faces a unique problem. Specifically, uniform program prescriptions cannot be offered. The rationale for this conclusion is quite simple: detailed plans cannot be provided before the intricacies of a community are investigated. Considering the idiosyncratic nature of health and illness, analysis should not proceed according to elaborate pre-established schemes. At best, therefore, reflexive guidelines of intervention can be proposed. In other words, ideas can be proffered for the purpose of expanding knowledge and cultural awareness.

Consistent with the critical thrust of reflexivity, access to the social world is expanded through the use of a reflexive model. Stated differently, this sort of model is not simply a heuristic device. Instead of concretizing particular conceptions of knowledge and order, the "epistemological thresholds" of these notions are recognized and expanded.[1] Translated into more concrete terms, the identities of persons, boundaries of organizations, and modes of administration, for example, are rendered fluid. As a result, the community is able to become an integral part of the intervention process.

Due to the prevalence of dualism in the past, most models have been underpinned by the theme of "increasing rationalization."[2] An explicit division of labor, exact organizational boundaries, and specialization with respect to the acquisition of knowledge are thought to enhance the formation and implementation of policies. Clearly this view is dubious, for the stasis and limited vision that are encouraged are seldom productive. This is particularly the case when something as dynamic as a community is supposed to be investigated.

A model that is community-based, instead, should foster the interpenetration of opposites. Concepts and principles that were formerly believed to be categorically separate should be viewed as united at their boundaries. For only when dualism is unchallenged, does a line of demarcation signal the presence of irreconcilable differences. In the absence of dualism, elements that are apparently contradictory can be merged without the fear that automatically reason and rigor must be jeopardized. Differences can be reconciled, in order to increase the responsiveness of interventions.

These differences have assumed many forms. Most obvious, considering the topic of this book, are the many cultural variations that exist. However, other styles of difference are also present. For example, organizations and their environments have been thought traditionally to occupy separate realms. Likewise, certain organizational roles are often presumed to be basically antagonistic. Yet as long as these and other dualisms persist, integrating intervention into communities will remain difficult. Management strategies, the demands imposed by roles, and organizational boundary maintenance may impede the delivery of services. Rather than relate indirectly to communities, agencies should actively "engage" those who are served.[3] The method of delivery, therefore, should not inadvertently establish the reality for intervention.

Overcoming the restrictions imposed by conceptual or programmatic schemes is a never ending adventure. Stated differently, a practitioner who is pluralistic and culturally sensitive should labor at the "boundary" of the clinical or organizational constructs that are used. While occupying this precarious position, differences, limitations, and culturally appropriate or relevant interventions can be recognized. Further, delivery programs should not be viewed as the final link in a massive social service system. Implied by this denial is that delivery actually begins at the nexus of agency and community, and thus this juncture should remain permeable.

In order to gain this kind of intimacy, a critical disposition toward premature closure should be maintained and a good deal of patience exercised. Specifically, the community should become increasingly inclusive as a guiding concept. Community-based practitioners, in short, should not envision the community as a narrowly conceived object of study. Indeed, planning and treatment, including all other facets of intervention, should be reviewed and inaugurated by a community. No differentiation should be made between service providers and the focus of treatment.

As should be noted, strong symbolism is associated with the idea of community. But, viewing clients to be "consumers" of services may or may not be an accurate analogy. To be a correct portrayal, clients should be able to participate fully in the selection and thus the creation of services. These persons, moreover, should be allowed to perform an entire repertoire of behaviors, which includes identifying and solving problems.

In fact, only recently has the role of "healer" been allotted solely to specialists. But technical experts do not have a monopoly on caring, and evidence suggests that they may not be very adept at this undertaking.[4] For as Joseph Weizenbaum rightly notes, caring, loving, and healing are not technical issues.[5] The point is that the range of skills necessary to address most problems can be found in practically every community, and thus directly stimulating, supporting, and utilizing these abilities should not sound odd. In order for this proposal to appear reasonable and efficient, however, several programmatic changes should receive serious consideration.

Modifying Traditional Roles

Role conflict has been a common theme in social service agencies. This notion was popularized by functionalists, who claimed that ambiguous role assignments cause problems in an organization. Unclear lines of authority, the duplication of effort, and conflicts of interest, for example, have been believed to lead naturally to inefficiency and ineffectiveness. So as to avoid these and related sources of difficulty, "job design" should be rigorous.[6] Any overlap in tasks should thus be avoided.

Due to the prevalence of this functionalist orientation, the fragmentation of agencies has been subtly encouraged. For instance, program evaluators have been kept separate from administrators, while medical personnel and outreach workers have occupied very different roles in a program.[7] Of course, social class and occupational prestige have contributed to this division of labor, for those who have spent most of their time contacting clients in the community have been activists and paraprofessionals.

On the other hand, psychiatrists have very limited contact with either the community or patients. Their role often consists of authorizing records and providing medication. Curiously, they remain essential to the operation of CMHCs, because they stand at the apex of professional decision making. Nonetheless, psychiatrists are not often an integral part of the healing process. They are an indispensable adjunct, who spend much of their time with paperwork and moving around service agencies because they hold multiple staff appointments.

Their special treatment sparked an insidious issue involved in creating the divisiveness that is found typically in social service agencies. That is, the members of various professions became concerned about their status within the scientific community.[8] What psychiatrists and psychologists were discovering was that applied science and politics are often related. Therefore, retaining their positions as "detached observers," or scientists, would become increasingly difficult.[9] The fundamental philosophical thrust of the community mental health movement, in other words, stipulated that social change should be an integral part of an intervention strategy. Obviously, making this a condition of successful intervention complicates the job of practitioners and transcends their traditional roles. Indeed, clearly establishing the requisite environment for a healthy life extends far beyond the traditional job descriptions of most psychiatrists and clinical psychologists.

When persons do things to others and try to alter situations, value judgments are operative. What could be more political than giving someone the latitude to manipulate another person's behavior? But due to professional role expectations, the explicit division of labor enforced in most agencies, and the accompanying desire to be scientific, practitioners have been slow to respond to the challenges posed by community-based intervention. In short, the fear of role conflict has prevented intervention from becoming truly comprehensive. By limiting themselves to the tasks associated with the principle of value-freedom, most of the activities of practitioners have remained marginal to the intervention process. The exciting and difficult aspects of intervention, which are instrumental to instituting substantial social change, reside outside the traditional purview of narrow guild perspectives and scientific protocol.

Transcending the restrictions imposed by the usual division of labor is necessary if community-based intervention can be expected to succeed. Nevertheless, the model found in most agencies is based on the belief that efficiency results from increased specialization. Once a task is sufficiently refined, extraneous factors are assumed to be eliminated that reduce productivity. Standardization and credentialism, in short, are thought to guarantee the integrity of both an organization and any undertaking.[10] Presupposed by this approach to job design is that a limited focus enables a few skills to be perfected, which are crucial to the survival of any business or agency.

Yet this method of structuring a program conflicts with the aim of community-based intervention. Rather than restricted, a practitioner's skills should extend beyond the range typically stipulated by professional or scientific standards. Within the context of community-based intervention, specialization may be a serious handicap. The belief should be fostered, accordingly, that efficiency does not necessarily decline because a practitioner is multidimensional. In fact, the ability to integrate apparently disparate roles is an asset. For rigidity reduces effectiveness when implementing a community-based program. Furthermore, a narrow mindset is not helpful when inaugurating a cross-cultural intervention.

Therefore, the practices that are supposed to enhance efficiency should be reevaluated by those who are committed to adopting interventions that are culturally sensitive. In this context, curtailing the options of practitioners in the name of efficiency does not make much sense. With respect to community-based intervention, inefficiency most often results when unexpected data are not handled deftly due to a lack of flexibility, and when practitioners do not have the political acuity required to get policies implemented. Clearly, strict adherence to standard role requirements will not correct these sources of error. What this means is that improved efficiency should come to be viewed as a product of flexibility.

Multidimensional Treatment

As discussed extensively in chapter four, mental health practitioners have been strongly encouraged to adopt the medical model. In actual practice, this has meant physicians are treated as the cornerstone of CMHCs. As Eliot Freidson writes, "Their mandate consists in defining whether a problem does or does not exist, what is 'truly' its nature, and how it should be tackled."[11] Typically, if a certain number of physician hours could not be secured, facilities would often have to close temporarily. In terms of treatment, medical doctors have been given the latitude traditionally to override the decisions made by psychologists or social workers. Obviously clients and the members of their families have been the last to be consulted in the treatment process.

The need to have physicians legitimize interventions has been so great that their opinions have been sought in areas where they clearly have lacked the expertise. Drug treatment provides a case in point. In the early days of drug intervention, particularly with heroin addicts, little was known about how treatment should proceed. Most often, whatever seemed to work with alcoholics was applied to other addicts. Gradually this strategy proved to be incorrect, for heroin users tend to view their problem much more in political and social terms. Nonetheless, physicians were placed in positions that allowed them to control treatment. As a result, methadone medication remained for a long time the primary treatment modality.

In the mid to late 1970s, a call was heard for multidisciplinary treatment planning. This approach was even recommended in the standards produced by the Joint Commission on Hospital Accreditation (JCAH).[12] Traditionally, however, this accreditation agency has been controlled by medical doctors and reflected the medical model. Programs that pass their rigorous review are assumed to be offering high quality services. Moreover, in many locations, receiving third-party payments has been linked to gaining and retaining JCAH approval. With the medical model tied so closely to funding services, how can the influence of physicians be expected to decline?

Recognition of the medical model has been guaranteed in another significant way. As is mentioned in chapter four, those who accredit agencies have usually required that each client's file contain a psychological report. As might be suspected, at the conclusion of a psychological assessment a DSM-III diagnosis is rendered. The fees that are charged for services, moreover, have been justified by the involvement of psychologists and psychiatrists in this activity. In fact, many third-party payers, such as insurance companies, will not reimburse a client or agency unless a clinical judgment that is supported by the DSM-III is made.

This demand places prevention and other so-called "ancillary services" in a precarious position. Specifically, how are these aspects of intervention supposed to be adequately funded? After all, "indirect" services are unrelated to the DSM-III diagnostic process. This funding strategy inadvertently provides any activity—along with particular staff persons—that is not related to direct services with an inferior and vulnerable status. Unfortunately, many of the tasks that are required by community-based intervention are classified in this manner. Considering that the Community Mental Health Act was passed over twenty years ago, how can this approach to funding be allowed to continue? Clearly a new funding mechanism is necessary, if the aim of this legislation is ever to be fulfilled.

The narrow focus of traditional intervention was supposed to be overcome through the use of multidisciplinary treatment teams. Accordingly, standards were proposed by JCAH for outpatient clinics that seemed to challenge, albeit minimally, the dominance of the medical model. By emphasizing the multidimensional character of intervention, increased sensitivity and insight were thought to be gained.

Reconstituting treatment teams in this way was supposed to change several key facets of intervention. First, and maybe foremost, the impact of physicians would hopefully be tempered. Providing equal status to every member of a treatment team was designed to foster this end. For example, social workers would no longer have to defer automatically to medical doctors. Physicians who have expertise in limited areas would be simply consulted when necessary, rather than monopolize every discussion. Their "guardianship status" would thus be revoked.[13]

Second, a holistic or multidimensional analysis would be encouraged, because the medical model would be placed in direct competition with other methodologies. As a result, the knowledge base used for making clinical decisions would likely expand. For possibly the first time physicians would have to make the case publicly that their remedies are most appropriate in any situation. In this way, every knowledge base would be placed on equal footing. Hence no claim can be identified as inherently better than any other. This maneuver means that clients, the members of their families, and a host of formerly disenfranchised practitioners can be encouraged to contribute input to a treatment plan.

Third, the range of tactics adopted to intervene in communities would probably expand, because medical practices would be subject to the same scrutiny as all others. Consequently, DSM-III diagnoses, for example, can be used in concert with a variety of social assessments. Because attention can be diverted from medical criteria, social correctives can be given a chance to succeed. In the field of drug abuse this shift occurred when serious questions began to be raised about the physiological basis of heroin addiction. A controversy ensued, which culminated in the model advanced by Dole and Nyswander losing prestige among many counselors.[14] Various interventions that are more socially oriented were thus discussed and adopted. Heroin use came to be viewed as a social phenomenon, rather than merely a medical issue.

This democratization of knowledge, however, is hardly complete. For instance, accreditation committees are still controlled by medical personnel. Further, everything from record keeping to client assessments is done by technicians. In many programs, this trend has become increasingly commonplace. Additionally, a DSM-III diagnosis remains vital to securing third-party payments. The power in most agencies, therefore, is lodged in a few hands. Criticizing physicians or clinical psychologists is a sensitive task, for these individuals can cause an agency's license to be revoked and funds to be lost. Thus debate does not often extend beyond a point that is acceptable to these professionals. Finally, the majority of practitioners appear to be enamored of psychological testing for many reasons. Prestige is associated with the ability to administer, score, and, particularly, interpret tests.[15] Testers are a valued commodity in agencies, for they are the handmaid to medical personnel and are thought to have access to information that has an aura of objectivity.

Due to these and other similar factors, multidisciplinary treatment planning has turned out to be no different from the style that was prevalent when physicians openly controlled this process. Physicians, clinical psychologists, and a host of recently created technical roles are central to treatment planning. Before progress can be made in this area, new approaches to accrediting agencies, billing for services, and legitimizing clinical and other judgments will have to be addressed. The conditions will have to be changed that discourage the use of diverse knowledge bases, or multidimensional treatment planning will not be widespread.

Action Research

Considering the theory of knowledge presupposed by community-based intervention, the research and evaluation process that guides program planning should be rethought. Particularly, researchers should become aware of what Polanyi calls the "tacit knowing" that occurs in a community.[16] This does not mean simply that so-called "key informants" should be contacted more frequently, or "community forums" should be conducted periodically to meet the program evaluation requirements imposed by states or the federal government. For most often the data collection instruments have been already developed, not to mention the research design and plan of analysis, long before the stage is reached where citizens have been asked to participate in evaluation studies.

Most policy research has been based on what might be called an elite model. Research, in this case, does not originate from the community. For example, the plans for operating a program are most often designed by federal or state officials. Usually program evaluation strategies are included as a part of these proposals. Moreover, data classification categories are created by government researchers to produce information to determine whether or not these abstract policies are working. Once the necessary data are garnered, they are sent to Washington, D.C. or a state capital where they are aggregated, analyzed, and incorporated into research reports. Eventually these findings are disseminated piecemeal to those who implement programs at the local level.

Another prominent form of this elitism relates to the use of consultants. Private firms that have contracts with the government, in addition to freelance researchers, have been instrumental in the formulation of policies and the implementation and evaluation of programs. Not only are these consultants rarely members of the communities they serve, their "boiler plate" approach to research is well-known. By this it is meant that they have a tendency to use similar research designs and theories to analyze any problem. A consulting firm may be visibly present in the field of drug abuse one month, and six months later, with the same methods, be providing advice to those who are planning detention facilities for juveniles. Identical methods, in short, are thought to be applicable to a wide range of issues. Although some knowledge is preferable to none, this approach overlooks the needs of special populations and has little value for identifying deficits in specific service modalities.

The result of this elite model is that relevant information is seldom made available, in a timely manner, to planners, administrators, and, particularly to those who provide direct services. Thus, policies often violate the aims of community members, such as when programs are placed in inaccessible locations or unwanted services are offered. Additionally, the "turn-around" time on government reports, especially those related to client follow-up, is so long that they are useless for making informed management decisions. Consultants are famous for coming into town one day and departing the next, and leaving behind recommendations that make little sense. In other words, this "top-down" approach has no utility in agencies that are community-based.

This elite model is especially ineffectual in minority communities. Input at the highest levels of the government bureaucracy is very limited to minorities. Sometimes a cabal of minority researchers is consulted, but the resulting input is minimal and is seldom representative of actual communities.

Furthermore, the number of minorities employed by consulting firms is very small, in addition to the fact that these companies are not noted for proposing idiosyncratic programs of research. The cost of providing new models for each of their clients is considered to be prohibitive. Overall the result is that method and technique are given precedence over securing relevant information. Quality is obscured by efficiency and expediency.

Quite some time ago Kurt Lewin supplied a remedy for this unsavory condition. He called this solution "action research."[17] What he meant by this phrase is that those who are studied should be included in every aspect of a research project. In this sense, the dualism that is present in the elite model is undermined. The asymmetry that exists usually between researchers and their subjects is subverted. Those who are investigated are given the ability to specify how this is done. Why should traditional researchers object to this practice?

Opponents of action research claim that client or subject involvement in a study contaminates the collection of data. This position, however, reflects dualism, for the belief is apparent that pure data can be obtained. For researchers who are culturally sensitive, the issue should not be whether interpretation constitutes a source of bias. Instead, most important should be to insure that a proper or socially significant interpretation of a situation is gained. Contamination occurs, accordingly, when irrelevant values or beliefs influence data collection. Excluding the members of a community from research activities should be understood to promote the adulteration of data.

What are some of the key components of action research? For instance, intimate collaboration should take place between researchers and the members of a community during the early stages of a project. The likelihood is thus improved that inappropriate research questions will be avoided. Furthermore, the strategies for contacting and interviewing persons, along with determining the most efficacious points of community entry, can be made more socially sensitive if citizens illustrate the parameters of the sampling universe and identify the relevant viewpoints. At another level, through the proper use of language and an understanding of decorum, interviews can become dialogical. The necessary rapport can be engendered, in other words, so that persons are not wary of interviewers.

Additionally, plans for analyzing data should not alter the information that is gathered. Statistical significance, for example, should be subordinate to questions of social relevance. To this end, citizens can assist in interpreting findings, thereby putting this information into a proper perspective. This is a variation of what Argyris calls "double-loop learning," whereby data are reformulated by the original subjects.[18] Also, the potential use of any data or reports can be discussed. Can persons be expected to divulge information, if they do not know how it will be used? The political nature of a specific study can be clarified through action research, in order to avert damaging a community. In the past, many communities have participated in research projects, only to have the data that were gathered misrepresented and researchers disappear.

In addition to facilitating methodological improvements, the obligations researchers have to a community can be detailed. Most important is that these experts should leave their skills behind, after they depart from a location. Indeed, the members of a community should be trained to undertake the research necessary to guide the interventions they need.

Their dependency should not increase, due to researchers assisting them in resolving an issue.

The purpose of action research is to create "emic" data collection instruments, analysis techniques, and training. Research is built from the "ground up." Gone is the hidden message of the elite model, which suggests that communities do not understand their own needs and require outside assistance to solve their problems. Congruent with the theoretical tenets of community-based or culturally oriented research, a community is not merely the focus of attention. Rather, those who are studied are thought to be best able to comprehend their situation, and participate in the generation of new knowledge and intervention tactics.

Community-Based Organizations

Every social agency has been required for some time to have an organizational chart. This description of an organization's structure has been part of most accreditation standards. In general, these charts have been very similar since their inception in service programs. Found most often has been a "scalar-chain" of authority, which means that most agencies have assumed the form of a bureaucracy.[19]

Accordingly, an extensive division of labor is outlined, along with clearly delineated lines of authority. The internal environment of the organization is neatly arranged, while access routes to the surrounding environs are explicitly specified. Furthermore, authority is arranged in a hierarchy. Every aspect of organizational life, in sum, is formalized.[20]

Problems associated with the internal environment of a bureaucracy will be raised first. The most pressing problem relates to the precise division of labor. As is required by this structure, everyone becomes a specialist. Consequently, little information is exchanged between persons or departments, as everyone remains ensconced within their own bailiwick. For allowing different information bases to be merged is thought to result in inefficiency. A practitioner who fails to adopt a specialty is likely to be viewed as having questionable utility or a nuisance. Conceptual myopia, reduced spontaneity, and the devaluation of creativity are consequences of bureaucratization. These are the outcome of what is sometimes called the "bureaucratic trap."[21] Clearly community-based intervention should be facilitated when these traits are either diminished or absent from an agency. In actual practice, the strictures imposed by a bureaucracy are usually overcome through the development of informal networks.

The authority pattern in a bureaucracy is also problematic. First, personal recognition and an increase in salary are by-products of vertical mobility. Certainly the reward mechanism that is present in these organizations does not encourage practitioners to stay involved in providing direct services. But a person's clinical skills are not likely to be broadened by following an administrative track! If anything, pursuing a career in administration results in stifling growth in other areas. As a rule, petty bureaucrats do not often make good therapists.

Also, professionalism and credentialism are rewarded in a bureaucracy. Movement up the hierarchy often requires advanced degrees and an ever increasing amount of specialized training. Little mobility, therefore, is available to paraprofessionals, while finding a way to reward volunteers is very difficult. What this means is that the persons who may know the most about a community, usually remain at the periphery of an agency. Hence intervention is guided inadvertently by those who may be least qualified, in terms of having the skills needed to enter a community.

Parenthetically, the hierarchical arrangement protects the status of physicians and other clinical experts.[22] Status differentials are easily maintained, because a significant amount of organizational distance is kept between these persons and other practitioners. A mystique can be associated with the knowledge and skills possessed by this caste of professionals, thereby centralizing intervention efforts.

By their very nature, bureaucracies are focused inward, for input must be restricted if efficiency is to be maintained. Boundary maintenance thus becomes extremely important. According to most organizational diagrams, therefore, agencies are mostly indirectly connected to the communities they serve. This occurs typically by impaneling a board of directors that supposedly has ties to the community. To use a phrase that has become quite popular, these individuals are supposed to serve as "cultural representatives."[23] Board members, stated differently, are expected to keep an agency in touch with a community. Nonetheless, the administrators of agencies are frequently disposed to choose a board that will insure their political survival. Hence no one is available to protect the interests of the community.

In fact, the influence of these so-called representatives has been minimal. Even the apparatuses that have been introduced to allow for community input have not been wisely utilized. For example, the time and location of board meetings are supposed to be advertised before these sessions are convened. But most often this requirement has not been taken seriously. One notice may be placed in a newspaper that is marginal to a community's key sources of information. As a result, attendance at these gatherings has been generally low, thereby indicating further to bureaucrats that community members are not interested in public affairs. When those who are not employed by an agency do attend, their presence has been given nominal attention. Surely the status differentials that are visible at these meetings do not encourage citizens to participate in discussions.

For the reasons just mentioned, various alternatives to bureaucracy should be given serious consideration by the administrators of agencies. These "flat" styles of organization, as they are sometimes called, allow standard roles to expand and promote flexible responses that are important to a community. To use Etzioni's typology, staff members are encouraged to become more than "emotionally" attached to an agency.[24] The philosophy that sustains this revolutionary move is that an organization can be regulated without rigid departmental boundaries and a hierarchy of authority. Moreover, once these barriers are dissolved, the prospects for good community relations are likely to improve.

Rensis Likert revealed an approach to developing a flat organization that is relevant to the task of structurally integrating agencies.[25] In this case, an organization is held together through a "linking-pin" strategy. Simply described, key members of each department are assigned to participate in the planning sessions conducted by other departments. Hence, departments that were formerly indirectly related are directly joined. A so-called informal network is developed to supplement the formal hierarchy.

Some of the benefits to be derived from this maneuver are as follows. First, merging different knowledge bases is relatively easy, once traditional organizational boundaries are no longer reinforced. Second, job rotation occurs as persons move from one department to another. Each employee is thus able to acquire a large number of skills and perform a wide range of tasks. Third, practitioners are rewarded for expanding laterally, rather than just vertically. At each level of an agency, a myriad of possibilities exist for personal involvement, recognition, and assuming increased responsibilities. What Randall Collins calls "bureaucratic violence" is reduced in a linking-pin organization, because the growth of employees is unrestricted.[26]

Equally important is that linking-pin organizations are permeable, due to the absence of a single line of authority. Community access is thus possible at every level. Some contemporary writers contend that this relationship between a community and organization resembles a "rhizome," because the lines of integration extend simultaneously in a number of directions.[27] The center of a flat agency is difficult to discern, because employees and community members unite and form different configurations based on the need to address a variety of issues. Subverted is the dualism that has been witnessed in the separation of individual needs from organizational demands, along with the schism that removes agencies from indigenous social networks. As a result, social agencies can be "decentered" and thoroughly democratized, for the community is envisioned as pervading an agency.

Training and Cultural Sensitivity

With only a few exceptions, the training practitioners have been receiving does not prepare them to operate effectively in communities or to become effective trainers.[28] Combined with the paucity of highly trained minority recruits, service delivery to ethnic communities has undoubtedly suffered. The problem is the community is only tangentially related to the instruction that has been received. Little integration has occurred, in other words, between the community and the educational philosophy and practice in colleges and universities.

At first this charge may not sound plausible. After all, field placements, practicums, and research opportunities have been a part of the curriculum provided by most graduate schools. Additionally, some professional associations have begun to require that issues pertaining to ethnicity be handled in a systematic manner. This is the case, for example, in any social work program that is accredited. What is wrong is that the community is treated as merely a resource to be used—sometimes referred to as a "laboratory"—and is not at the core of training. Therefore, the values associated with community-based intervention do not underpin the curriculum. Nor are the organizational means in place that allow significant input from the community to be interjected into the training process.

For instance, acquiring research skills constitutes a large part of the education received by practitioners. Yet how much of this training is relevant to the actual problems they confront in the community or has a significant ethnomethodological thrust?[29] Most often instruction has proceeded as usual, with students learning about sampling, experimental and quasi-experimental designs, data collection and analysis, and the presentation of findings. What informs this training are the presuppositions of positive science, rather than ethnography. As a result, the community is approached as a sort of "data bank," rather than a concept that completely changes the nature of research. But promoting a facsimile of traditional university research should not be the aim of community-based training.

When the community is ubiquitous to the education of practitioners, technical and social concerns should no longer be kept separate. The worth of a particular methodology should be assessed in terms of its utility in a specific setting, rather than standard protocol. In short, questions related to procedural issues should be raised in the context of the community. Thus a different ethic guides training than is usually the case. This ethic is perverted, however, if the focus of attention is simply the desire to solve logistical problems that are a part of doing applied science. Instead, the thrust of training should shift to viewing the community as supplying the necessary framework for all methodological discussions.

Obviously another curriculum matter that should be addressed pertains to the inclusion of material related to minorities. This does not mean discussing at various times throughout a course the cultural heritage or alleged idiosyncracies of different ethnic groups. Much more important, epistemological questions should be raised concerning the role of language in shaping reality. Moreover, the fact that culture mediates thoroughly intervention should be appreciated. Here, again, the influence of culture should not be simply one more topic that is covered. Rather, culture should be another unifying theme of the curriculum.

In a more practical vein, members of the community should be allowed to participate directly in the education of practitioners. Usually this concern is addressed by granting adjunct faculty status to certain professionals who live or work in the community. However, these persons have been used mostly to supervise field placements. Rarely have they been actually permitted to teach courses or participate in making the decisions that affect the curriculum. For the structure of most universities does not invite the collaboration between faculty members and citizens that is necessary for socially relevant training to occur.

While continuing this theme of the community as a knowledge base for orienting instruction, students may benefit greatly from moving outside of the classroom. Classes and practicums could be held in storefronts, civic centers, multiservice agencies, the homes of community members, or other locations where meetings can take place. The point is to retain students in the community as long as possible. Making contacts, learning about the nature of informal social networks, and becoming familiar with important institutions is almost a full-time job. Actually studying in the community can make easier the necessary immersion in culture.

The training that is vital to preparing practitioners to enter communities should extend beyond what is available in most professional schools. Often the education provided in these places has been fragmented, for the curriculum usually has consisted of courses that have been related only because they are part of a single discipline, or have been viewed as belonging to a set of cognate fields of study. Also missing have been appropriate role models, for social activists have been rare among the individuals found on the faculties of professional schools. Intensive community involvement has not been rewarded, and nor has activism been thought to be an essential part of science. The traditional training received by professionals has been fairly conservative due to the lack of emphasis that has been placed on epistemological critique, cultural differences, and political analysis. As was suggested earlier, becoming a true "cultural broker" seems to conflict with the calling of a professional.

Becoming a cultural broker is not easy. As noted correctly by Lefley and Bestman, these persons must overcome biases, including those indigenous to science, in order to fuse perspectives that appear to be very different.[30] Suggested throughout this book is that this is not just a scientific undertaking. Becoming culturally aware, accordingly, does not occur simply because a few obvious traits of a particular cultural group are recognized. Appreciably more significant, the "life-plan" of a community should be grasped, as described by Schutz.[31] As part of this process, the many dimensions that affect the generation of problems and are thus essential to intervention, are given a prominent position in the education of practitioners.

For example, the world of minority adolescents should be entered. This includes appreciating their family existence, peer relations, school experiences, and how these factors may be intertwined. Such a world, moreover, is anything but static. Hence the motivation for change should also be understood. In sum, being an adolescent in a minority community, or for that matter any community, is not a condition that consists of several well-circumscribed traits. Instead, the world of these persons is comprised of various zones of experience, each of which supplies criteria for interpreting behavioral expectations.

Conclusion

After reading this chapter, the close association between knowledge, culture, and power should be obvious.[32] Becoming a practitioner who is culturally sensitive requires that a critical eye be directed to each of these items. Bureaucratically reinforced power, for instance, should not be permitted to block access to a community or make obsolete the training of community-based practitioners. Likewise, the power associated with scientific knowledge should not be allowed to discredit the knowledge base of a community. Also, politics should not be viewed as anathema to science.

This attempt at integration brings to fruition anti-dualism. But most practitioners still do not view science as associated with power, because scientists are supposedly value-free. Similarly, what does reliable knowledge have to do with culture? Culture is assumed to be based traditionally on values, while true knowledge consists of facts. That assumptions made about knowledge can affect how agencies are organized, treatment is arranged, and the relationship between a service program and the community is structured, may initially seem improbable to many practitioners. Nonetheless, those who want to adopt a community-based orientation should be sensitive to how facts, values, and the ability to either accurately apprehend or misconstrue the meaning of behavior are interrelated.

Notes

1. Deleuze, Gilles. *Foucault*. (Minneapolis: University of Minnesota Press, 1986), p. 51.
2. Weber, Max. *Economy and Society*, vol. 2. (Berkeley: University of California Press, 1978), pp. 1115–1116.
3. Sartre, Jean-Paul. *What is Literature*? (New York: Washington Square Press, 1986).
4. Karger, Howard Jacob and Larry W. Kreuger. "Technology and the 'Not Always so Human' Services." In *Technology and Human Service Delivery*, ed. John W. Murphy and John T. Pardeck. (New York: The Haworth Press, 1988), pp. 111–116.
5. Weizenbaum, Joseph. *Computer Power and Human Reason*. (San Francisco: W.H. Freeman, 1976), p. 270.
6. Murphy, John W. "Organizational Issues in Worker Ownership," *American Journal of Economics and Sociology*, 43(3), 1984, pp. 287–299.
7. Patton, Michael Quinn. *Practical Evaluation*. (Beverly Hills, CA: Sage, 1982), pp. 304–305; Weiss, Carol. *Evaluation Research*. (Englewood Cliffs, NJ: Prentice-Hall, 1972), pp. 98–102.
8. Sabshin, Melvin, "The Anti-Community Mental Health 'Movement'," *American Journal of Psychiatry*, 125(8), 1969, pp. 41–47.
9. Toulmin, Stephen. *The Return to Cosmology: Postmodern Science and the Return to Cosmology*. (Berkeley: University of California Press, 1982).
10. Collins, Randall. *The Credential Society*. (New York: Academic Press, 1979).
11. Friedson, Eliot. *Profession of Medicine: A Study in the Applied Sociology of Knowledge*. (New York: Dodd and Mead, 1970), p. 205.
12. Popko, Kathleen. *Regulatory Controls*. (Lexington, MA: D.C. Health and Company, 1976), pp. 27–28.
13. Castel, Robert. *The Regulation of Madness*. (Berkeley: University of California Press, 1988), p. 189.
14. Beschner, George and James M. Walters. "Just Another Habit? The Heroin User's Perspective on Treatment." In *Life with Heroin*, ed. Bill Hansen, George Beschner, James M. Walters, and Elliott Bovelle. (Lexington, MA: D.C. Health and Company, 1985), pp. 155–173.
15. Matarazzo, Joseph. "Computerized Clinical Test Interpretations: Invalidated Plus All Mean and No Sigma," *American Psychologist*, 41(1), 1986, pp. 14–24.
16. Polanyi, Michael. *The Tacit Dimension*. (New York: Doubleday, 1967), p. 4.

17. Argyris, Chris, Robert Putnam, and Diana McLain Smith. *Action Science*. (San Francisco: Jossey-Bass, 1985).

18. Ibid., p. 53.

19. Abrahamsson, Bengt. *Bureaucracy or Participation*. (Beverly Hills, CA: Sage, 1977), pp. 15–33.

20. Perrow, Charles. *Complex Organizations*. (New York: Random House, 1986), pp. 1–48.

21. Kantner, Rosabeth Moss. *The Change Masters*. (New York: Simon and Schuster's Sons, 1983), p. 137.

22. Castel, Robert. *The Regulation of Madness*, pp. 191–218.

23. Lefley, Harriet P. "Delivering Mental Health Services Across Cultures." In *Mental Health Services: The Cross-Cultural Context*, ed. Paul B. Pedersen, Norma Sartorius, and Anthony J. Marsella. (Beverly Hills, CA: Sage, 1984), pp. 135–171.

24. Etzioni, Amitai. "Organizational Control Structure." In *Handbook of Organizations*, ed. James G. March. (Chicago: Rand McNally, 1965).

25. Likert, Rensis. *New Patterns of Management*. (New York: McGraw-Hill, 1961), pp. 113–115.

26. Collins, Randall. "Three Faces of Cruelty: Toward A Comparative Sociology of Violence." In *Sociology Since Midcentury*, by Randall Collins. (New York: Academic Press, 1981), pp. 133–158.

27. Deleuze, Gilles and Felix Guattari. *On the Line*. (New York: Semiotex(e), 1983).

28. Casas, J. Manuel. "Making Effective Use of Research to Impact the Training of Culturally Sensitive Mental Health Workers." In *Mental Health Research and Practice in Minority Communities: Development of Culturally Sensitive Training Programs*, ed. Manuel R. Miranda and Harry H.L. Kitano. (Rockville, MD: National Institute of Mental Health, 1986), pp. 117–131.

29. Garfinkle, Harold. *Studies in Ethnomethodology*. Englewood Cliffs, NJ: Prentice–Hall, 1967).

30. Lefley, Harriet P. and Evalina W. Bestman. "Community Mental Health and Minorities: A Multi-Ethnic Approach." In *The Pluralistic Society*, ed. Stanley Sue and Thom Moore. (New York: Human Sciences Press, 1984), pp. 116–148.

31. Schutz, Alfred. *Collected Papers, Vol III*. (The Hague: Nijhoff, 1966), p. 122.

32. Foucault, Michel. *Knowledge/Power*. (New York: Pantheon Books, 1980).

Chapter Eight

The Political Side of Community-Based Policies

Discourse and Politics

In the previous chapters, several key issues that have prevented the onset of true community-based intervention are addressed. The criticisms that are provided are mostly theoretical and organizational in thrust. Although political themes are presupposed by this discussion, they are not the focus of attention. A serious analysis of intervention, however, is impossible without devoting serious attention to how policies are shaped by politics. Given the current political climate, is community-based intervention likely to occur?

Nonetheless, what is offered in this chapter is not the standard diatribe against conservatives and their obvious support for those who are most economically powerful in this society. Certainly economic power is important to understanding the lack of equity in the distribution of health care. However, merely a change in political leadership may be insufficient to spawn widespread interest in community-based intervention. Nowadays the political rhetoric of democrats and republicans has become astonishingly similar. What needs to be addressed, instead, is the type of political discourse that can begin to change attitudes about this issue. For political influence is not simply related to the overt exercise of power, but additionally based on the ability to control how debate proceeds.

Michel Foucault made this point most forcefully.[1] He argues that changes in the nature of political discourse do not follow automatically from political shifts. Determinism such as this is naive and provides little insight into how alterations in social life are promoted. Before certain innovations will be tried, these developments must be viewed as rational and socially appropriate. In short, political inspiration does not necessarily supply these prerequisites. Various assumptions about reality must be abandoned, before alternative social arrangements will seem appealing.

To use Foucault's phrase, the range of "discursive formations" has remained quite stable for at least twenty years, for even at the height of the rebelliousness exhibited during the 1960s many of these ideas were not seriously challenged.[2] Mainstream politicians, both liberal and conservative, were and still are enmeshed within a similar style of discourse. Simply put, a particular outlook is adhered to by the members of both groups. In some circles, these assumptions about reality are referred to as constituting a world-view.

Yet dispersing the accouterments of power, for example, may be insufficient to expand the limits of dialogue. As is suggested throughout this book, reflexivity is essential to this task. But most politicians are realists and thus are thoroughly unreflexive. Their usual *modus operandi* is to adapt to the dominant political reality. Therefore, the proliferation of discourse is not likely to originate from these persons.

This chapter will illustrate how various themes indigenous to the prevailing range of discourse are incompatible with intervention that is culturally sensitive and are unlikely to foster support for the resources necessary to insure effective service delivery. As a result of demonstrating the parameters and restricted applicability of these ideas, expanded discussions are made possible about how intervention should proceed. Therefore, persons should not be reluctant to embrace community-based strategies, simply because they are typically thought to lack justification and be inherently unproductive. By exposing the presuppositions of the currently accepted discursive practices, community-based or culturally sensitive intervention may appear to be a necessary response to meeting human needs.

Although not openly confrontational, this maneuver is certainly political. Persons, situations, and institutions are subject to change. Once the justification for a particular political strategy is weakened, other options may gain momentum. What could be more political than undermining the legitimacy of a particular social reality? In fact, exposing hidden themes may be more revolutionary than simply attacking public figures and institutions. As some modern writers note, political efficacy has far more to do with maintaining legitimacy than with exhibiting force.[3]

Laissez-Faire Interaction

Central to political landscape of the 1980s has been a belief in laissez-faire economics. Supply-side critics argue, in a manner similar to classical theorists, that overt attempts to manipulate buying and selling are counterproductive. Their view is that no one possesses the knowledge necessary to regulate effectively the entire economy. Therefore, the forces of the market should be allowed to determine who prospers and fails. Past attempts to stimulate or repress aggregate demand are thought to have produced inflation, reduced incentives to invest, and stifled productivity.[4]

In general, advocates of the policy of laissez-faire are suspicious of intervention into any aspect of social life. Unfettered competition is thought to result in an optimal distribution of goods and services. Implied by this viewpoint is that rewards will gravitate to where they belong, if the natural operation of the marketplace is not disrupted.

Obviously overlooked by this position is the role that disparity in incomes, various forms of discrimination, and coercion play in the distribution of success in this society. Why should those who lack power believe that they will benefit from allowing those who already have vast resources to dominate the marketplace? In point of fact, the concept of social services is antagonistic to the principle of laissez-faire. Because competition is not fair, and outcomes are skewed in favor or those who are advantaged, intervention is believed to be necessary to ameliorate the resulting social conditions. Since the emphasis has been placed on competition, individualism, and personal motivation, the public has been convinced that intervention is deleterious. An "amoral" orientation has been spawned, because a concern for the commonweal is given a low priority.

Mobilizing social forces to correct public ills, therefore, is commonly assumed to be irrational. If problems are noticed, charity and voluntary organizations are thought to be sufficient correctives. The idea that relief can be produced only through systematic planning and intervention is not given much credence. But because social obligation and duty are not necessarily a part of the laissez-faire philosophy, how can volunteerism and other individualized measures be expected to have significant impact?

"Privatization" of Health Care

In recent years, the privatization of a variety of services has been encouraged.[5] This trend has been most visible in the field of corrections, although the privatization of other social services is underway. The operative rationale is that private firms can provide services more efficiently and effectively than government agencies. Assumed is that the government is bureaucratic, while privately owned companies are not. Moreover, in the absence of bureaucracy, the entrepreneurial spirit is thought to flourish.

Most important is that through privatization the public is sent a dubious message. Specifically, solving social problems is not a collective responsibility! Most citizens should live their lives as usual, while a select group of persons is given the charge to identify and correct difficulties. Public commitment for large-scale intervention is unlikely, as long as privatization is touted to be a panacea for social problems. But absolving citizens of their social responsibilities appears to be an untenable policy. How can a society be expected to survive, except in the most perverse form, without widespread and direct involvement from its members?

Also, the fundamental motive for privatization is economic. Facilities are thought to be built faster and run more effectively by private entrepreneurs. Yet can these firms be expected to undertake the type of interventions recommended by community-based practitioners? After all, these strategies are complex and not readily amenable to standardization. The type of production schedule required to increase profits may be anathema to interventions that are culturally sensitive. In short, these interventions should not be evaluated simply in terms of their efficiency. Other criteria, which are tangentially related to the business world, may be more pertinent. Indeed, in an area that is extremely labor intensive efficiency is difficult to estimate.

Social Services as Commodities

For the most part, in the United States, persons have been expected to pay a fee for their services. Health care, in other words, has been purchased like any other commodity.[6] If an individual has sufficient economic resources, the delivery of health services poses no significant problem. Additionally, group insurance rates have been offered by many companies so that employees can afford medical and other sorts of care.

Nonetheless, coverage is becoming increasingly costly, at a time when co-payments are being raised and government programs are being reduced. Comprehensive health care is becoming a luxury that is beyond the reach of more and more persons, especially for members of minority groups. For example, for those who subsist at the poverty level—a group that has increased over the past decade—prevention is a service that is seldom available. Visits to a doctor are made reluctantly and only when a crisis point has been reached.

In addition to the logistical problems inherent to the present approach to funding services, ethical issues are posed that are becoming increasingly pressing. That is, health care is linked to economic success! As a by-product of competing satisfactorily in the marketplace, a person has a right to health care. Insuring that the nation remains healthy is thus not a collective responsibility. In recent years, various governmental officials have stated openly that a healthy existence is not something citizens should be guaranteed. Most persons should not expect to receive regularly a full range of services, because, like a large house and other material assets, adequate health care is simply beyond the reach of a large segment of the citizenry.

This viewpoint becomes patently obvious when government programs are criticized for providing merely handouts, as if maintaining a person's health is merely a frivolous activity. As long as this attitude prevails, how will intervention ever be adequately funded? If economic opportunities are not adequately distributed across all segments of society, the health of many will be jeopardized. But should the receipt of health care depend on the vagaries of the marketplace? Clearly this is not a very humane policy. Actually a healthy existence is a prerequisite for economic success, and thus high quality services should be distributed throughout society. In this sense, health care is not a commodity, but something that should be supplied to insure the optimal functioning of society. The maintenance of health, in short, should not be left to chance by any society that wants to improve the productivity of all its members.

"Realism" and the Lack of Social Commentary

Social criticism has been silenced in the past few years. No one seems to be interested any longer in reforming society, because personal success may be jeopardized. Persons are simply not willing to risk their careers. Accordingly, much time is spent identifying social expectations and figuring out how to fulfill these demands most effectively. What might be called social "realism" has come to be accepted as normative. Particular conditions have been recognized as necessary, while intelligent persons learn how to navigate their way through the social system.

Nowadays critics are almost embarrassed to suggest that entire areas of the social system need to be transformed. The ideology of realism has become so pervasive that activists are viewed as hopelessly naive or romantics who have failed to acknowledge the end of the 1960s. Either way, sweeping proposals are considered to be irresponsible and unworkable. Obviously this lack of nerve has dire consequences for those who are socially disenfranchised.

Yet essential to the success of community-based interventions are novel plans. Practitioners who are community-based should be innovative and willing to try untested strategies. Gaining access to communities and creating culturally sensitive methodologies sometimes requires that unorthodox practices be adopted. Those who are reluctant to take risks and explore novel suggestions—question the prevailing status quo—will not likely be successful at this type of intervention. Therefore, the possible range of experiences and insights should not be truncated by realism. Realism should not be allowed to suppress imagination.

The Role of Social Scientists as "Value-Free"

Traditionally social practitioners have desired to be value-free. As a result, they have become a handmaid to science. A more precise account would be that practitioners have become technicians, who strive to avoid making judgments about the relevance of values to interventions. These so-called qualitative factors are thought to impede the discovery of facts and rational decision making. Debate is thus turned inward, and is focused primarily on methodological and other logistical problems. What this means is that technical competence has become the most visible measure of professionalism.

Methodological insensitivity is not the only shortcoming of attempting to transform social practice into technique. Most important for community-based intervention, practitioners must abandon their role of providing commentary and social criticism. In fact, rather than trying to formulate a critical perspective, practitioners have become satisfied to perform methodological tasks in policy research. Thus, the guidance of projects has been turned over inadvertently to those who merely expedite the research process.

Value-freedom and community-based intervention, however, should be seen as incompatible. Facts do not merely embody reality, but must be interpreted. Accordingly, bringing a proper interpretation to the forefront is not necessarily a scientific task. Exposing facts does not mean that they will be recognized, given credence, and utilized. Recognizing and putting information into practice, therefore, is not a value-free activity. Particular positions are challenged and rejected, while other views are adopted. Anyone who accepts a passive or value-free role in this process will be ineffectual. For judgments must be made and positions advanced, based on claims that often appear to be idiosyncratic. In this regard, facts and various procedures must be imbued with relevance. Hence advocacy and science should not be approached as antagonistic by community-based practitioners.

Biology, Individualism, and Reductionism

Throughout this book the "medical model" has been severely criticized. Therefore, the reductionistic character of this mode of conceptualization does not need to be reiterated at this juncture. But at this time, a related theme needs to be addressed. As a consequence of explaining social problems in biological terms, individualism is stressed. Social issues, as Mills suggested, are equated with personal faults or maladaptation.[7]

What kinds of interventions are appropriate when primacy is given to individualism? The point is that all interventions must be ahistorical. For if the individual is believed to be the source of most problems, the effects of sexism, racism, and other forms of institutional discrimination are not seen as worthy of attention. The focus of interventions can thus be extremely narrow, because the complex relationship between personal motives and social practices can be ignored.

This conception of intervention has far reaching policy implications. First of all, social critique is presumed to be irrelevant. What does society have to do with the individual psyche? Second, any intervention that is proposed must emphasize building coping skills. After all, proposing structural or social changes should only be a last resort. Third, the goal of empowering clients would be considered irrational, for the basic existence of these individuals is thought to be problematic. The question can be easily asked, why should power be given to these unfortunate individuals? For their ability to act reasonably or normally has become a point of contention.

The Technological Mentality

As Jacques Ellul points out, a "technological ethic" has come to pervade modern society.[8] By this he means that technologically based knowledge is viewed to be more valid than any other type. Materialism, quantification, and technical reason are uncritically accepted as essential to describing reality. According to this ethic, transforming judgments into technical protocol is thought to eliminate errors and improve the quality of any task. Formalizing a job in this way is assumed to improve the effectiveness and efficiency of any task.

However, as Ellul also notes, once the technological ethic is accepted, moral and other more qualitative issues are suppressed. Moral questions, simply put, are not precise and readily quantified. In fact, the pursuit of accuracy and truth is assumed to be hampered by the introduction of these speculative elements. For classificatory schemes are challenged and unsettled, thereby preventing the mechanistic cataloguing of events. But along with the suppression of moral queries, solutions that are not technically oriented are also eschewed. "Nontechnical" proposals are not thought to possess the rigor necessary for them to be effective. Correctives that deviate from the technological imperative are dismissed as lacking rationality. But changing the orientation of policies to meet the needs of minorities is not a technical issue!

Currently interventions are typically restricted to technological "fixes." Taken for granted is the present delivery system, and thus practitioners are merely given the latitude to make minor adjustments in how an agency operates. Asking whether service delivery is fair or just, not to mention questioning the equity of social relationships, is beyond the scope of the technological ethic. Yet assessing the adequacy of an agency is a value-based project! Goals or standards are predicated on expectations that are not necessarily technical. Obviously limiting intervention to making technical recommendations can result in obscuring the human dimension of service delivery. But how can technical criteria alone serve to guide an intervention? Fundamentally intervention is predicated on improving the quality of life, and obviously the human condition extends far beyond the realm of the technological.

The Idea that Nothing Works

In a now infamous article, Martinson declared that social programs have been a dismal failure.[9] "Almost nothing works," in short, and thus the government should no longer support large-scale interventions. The cost is simply too high, and the results are minimal. This has been the credo of the Reagan Administration, and thus most Americans have come to accept this position as factual. Even though critics of every political stripe have questioned Martinson's findings, his opinions have come to be recognized as prudent. Because interventions are futile, a permanent "underclass" is now reluctantly acknowledged to be a part of American society.

Obviously this sort of fatalism is antagonistic to the idea of intervention. This is not the time to refute Martinson's claims, for this has been done elsewhere, but to suggest that "nothing works" is more of a political statement than a conclusion based on unequivocal data.[10] Definitions, expectations, research methods, and a shifting political climate all affect how the impact of programs is evaluated. Therefore, the public should not be so gullible and underestimate the influence of hidden political and methodological predispositions on policy making.

Both in terms of formal and informal measures, communities have benefitted from social programs. Varying degrees of success have been reported. Yet most important, there is no reason why interventions are destined to fail. After all, the present undesirable social conditions have been created by various policies, and thus these trends can be reversed by dedicated persons. If the political will can be summoned, improvements can be brought about in minority and other communities. But these interventions will not be taken seriously until the malaise that has overcome this society is shed. The current reluctance to intervene in social life must be shown to be an ideology, rather than the outcome of historical evidence alone. Conclusive data have not been produced to justify the claim that interventions are a complete waste of money, despite the naive views that have been perpetrated.

Social Programs as a Method for Social Control

To many citizens, social service programs are understood to be a component of the correctional system. With the emphasis that has been placed on "law and order" for two decades, this association is not surprising. As the definition of criminal behavior expands, an increasing number of persons are either incarcerated or diverted into rehabilitation programs. Those who cannot be handled by the courts—and these are overwhelmingly members of minority groups—simply are understood to be appropriate for placement in community facilities.

The creation of this relationship in the mind of the public is unfortunate. Are intervention and incarceration synonymous? Only recently has this association come to be viewed as valid. Clearly incarceration is a means of social control, but interventions, particularly those that are truly community-based, do not perform this function. In fact, just the opposite is supposed to occur. Simply put, through interventions social conditions are supposed to be changed, so that persons can lead productive lives. Rather than controlling individuals, the intention should be to provide new opportunities.

Nonetheless, someone who needs help has come to be equated with a deviant or a threat to order. So even when rehabilitation is undertaken, as opposed to overt social control, the usual expectation is conformity in the guise of "adequate social functioning." Order is simply reified. On the other hand, order is defied by real intervention, for providing assistance is intended to help persons to develop, and development is often idiosyncratic and can proceed in any number of directions. Growth, in short, does not necessarily respect outmoded institutional or political imperatives.

Government Involvement and Inefficiency

At this time, skepticism surrounds the public funding of programs. In point of fact, every year an award is given to the most ridiculous federal program, in order to illustrate government waste. Many citizens have come to view these programs to be the product of "pork barrel" politics, because patronage and cronyism appear to be the rule. Because of the blatant mismanagement that seems to be rampant, distrust of the government is now commonplace. Accordingly, the government is thought to have a minor role in correcting social problems.

But some problems are so extensive that they cannot be addressed solely by local municipalities. In many cases, without federal resources and leadership the proper correctives may never be forthcoming. Nonetheless, the way in which projects have been planned, funded, and implemented is inefficient. Yet this does not signal that government intervention is inherently unproductive, as some visible critics of publicly funded programs claim.[11] However, the procedure for evaluating and implementing projects definitely needs to be revised.

At this time, a cabal of administrators and researchers, who mostly are not members of a minority group, determine who receives funding and the type of projects that are inaugurated. Because these persons also compete for funds, those who are in this group are often reluctant to criticize one another. On the surface competition for money may appear to be open and fair, but behind the scenes manipulation occurs and a grant proposal can be easily sabotaged or facilitated by the assignment of reviewers. As a result, funds are controlled by a small number of individuals who seldom admit newcomers.

Due to this situation, how can communities have input into the procurement of programs? In view of this increasing concentration of power, mental health programs that are innovative and sensitive to a community's needs are not likely to be supported. Therefore, new approaches to soliciting, approving, and implementing projects should be generated. Input from a wide range of sources should be sought, as well as improved communication with the representatives of minority communities. In sum, procedures should be made available to guarantee that planning is more comprehensive, and that all theories, models, and proposals are publicly corroborated.

Program Evaluation and Accountability

Apparently new funds are going to be made available by ADAMHA to evaluate programs and provide technical assistance.[12] Perhaps accountability is going to be a vogue topic once again, for this is not the first time that money has been earmarked for this purpose. Back in 1975, with the passage of P.L. 94-63, special funds were to be set aside for conducting program evaluation. Yet what has been the result of this effort?

For the most part, minimal evaluation standards were established at the local level. Often one or two simple needs assessment techniques, for example, were undertaken to guide service delivery. Most often, due to the procedure for allocating funds, the responsibility for evaluation was left to the community mental health board within a catchment area. As a result, needs assessments, trial experiments of treatment modalities, and follow-up studies were conducted with samples that had little relevance to individual programs or communities. Clearly the day-to-day management of an agency is not necessarily improved by this practice.

If new money is going to be devoted to program evaluation, care must be taken to insure that these funds are not devoured by a local bureaucracy. Community groups, instead, should be organized and allowed to monitor the spending of this money for needs assessments. The proper scope of this research can thus be publicly verified, while needs can be properly identified. With regard to the management of programs, enough money should be allocated so that individual agencies can inaugurate a comprehensive evaluation program. Hence information can be made available so that timely and, thus, accurate management decisions are possible. In short, injecting more money into an unresponsive local bureaucracy is only likely to arouse the ire of the public.

Bureaucracy Versus Innovation

The reward structures that are currently operative are antagonistic to community-based intervention. Most often persons are rewarded for following instructions and fulfilling organizational expectations. In a typical bureaucratic fashion, mobility is reserved for those who accept norms pertaining to the usual rate of production, do not challenge authority, and acknowledge the worth of traditional policies. Criticism and innovativeness are clearly discouraged.

To counteract this tendency, funds should be set aside to finance untested ideas. Instead of focusing on description and classification, more research that is driven by novel intervention theory should be given consideration. Rather than spin-off projects based on well-worn hypotheses, new starting points should be encouraged. Specifically, projects that have strong cultural components should not be devalued because of their apparent lack of scientific rigor. Instead of everyone protecting restricted areas of research, raising broader questions should be rewarded. The traditional piecemeal approach to research, in short, should be replaced by a more integrated, global and enlightened perspective.

Usually having a track record, proposing a project that fits into traditional funding cycles, working with well-known concepts and methods, and having the endorsement of others who have been awarded grants are vital to obtaining support from the government or private foundations. Clearly minorities are at a disadvantage in this process. No wonder so much research is stale or redundant! In order to remedy this condition, the usual safeguards adopted to insure that ideas are legitimate and researchers constitute a safe risk should be rethought. As long as novelty and speculation are viewed with suspicion, little advancement will be made in the area of community interventions. Using criteria that divert attention away from the unknown may be safe, but safety can suffocate creativity.

Conclusion

Unless these discursive practices are challenged, community-based intervention will be given a low priority. In all likelihood, intervention will be either unproductive or disruptive, due to the restrictive criteria that are invoked to guide this activity. Hence a new social context should be established, where enhancing the general welfare is thought to be an admirable goal. In this sense, active involvement in creating a healthy society will not be viewed as undermining personal initiative and the incentives that are believed to motivate persons.

Even worse, however, if these old ideologies are not discarded, community-based intervention may end up being nothing more than another means of social control. Some writers argue that this has already occurred.[13] Social control has simply become more unobtrusive, with CMHCs and private agencies replacing state hospitals as the key means of restraint. Unless changes are made in conceptualizing illness, and citizens are integral to this process, even community-based interventions may merely serve to identify and rehabilitate deviants.

Nonetheless, interventions that are community-sensitive are supposed to be liberating. Clients are supposed to be given a modicum of control over their lives, as a result of having the ability to regulate every aspect of their treatment. Although much lip service is paid nowadays to the idea of personal and community autonomy, the prerequisites for this autonomy have not been fulfilled. Until intervention becomes socially appropriate, many barriers will remain to creating a healthy society.

Notes

1. Foucault, Michel. *Discipline and Punish.* (New York: Pantheon, 1979).

2. Foucault, Michel. *The Archaeology of Knowledge.* (London: Tavistock, 1922), p. xxii.

3. Murphy, John W. *Postmodern Social Analysis and Criticism.* (Westport, CT: Greenwood, 1989), pp. 127–149.

4. Murphy, John W. "Conservative Economics and the Issue of Social Order at the Marketplace." In *Current Perspectives in Social Theory*, ed. John Wilson and Scott G. McNall. (Greenwich, CT: JAI Press, 1986), pp. 69–86.

5. Hutto, T. Don. "The Privatization of Prisons." In *Twenty Years of Correctional Reform: Are Prisons Any Better?* ed. John W. Murphy and Jack E. Dison. (Newbury Park, CA: Sage, 1990), pp. 111–127.

6. Turner, Bryan S. *Medical Power and Social Knowledge.* (Newbury Park, CA: Sage, 1987), pp. 200–202.

7. Mills, C. Wright. *The Sociological Imagination.* (London: Oxford University Press, 1959).

8. Ellul, Jacques. *The Technological Society.* (New York: Random House, 1964), pp. 127–128.

9. Martinson, Robert. "What Works?—Questions and Answers About Prison Reform," *The Public Interest* 35(Spring), 1974, pp. 22–54.

10. Palmer, Ted. *Correctional Intervention and Research.* (Lexington, MA: D.C. Health and Company, 1978).

11. Gilder, George. *Wealth and Poverty.* (New York: Basic Books, 1981).

12. "Bench Notes," *The Journal of NIH Research.* Sept-Oct, 1989, p. 124.

13. Lewis, Dan A., et al. *Worlds of the Mentally Ill.* (Carbondale, IL: Southern Illinois University Press, 1990).

Selected Annotated Bibliography

Binswanger, Ludwig. *Being-in-the-World.* New York: Basic Books, 1963. The work of Heidegger is invoked to create a socially sensitive mode of therapy (*Daseinanalyse*).

Blalock, Hubert M. *Conceptualization and Measurement in the Social Sciences.* Beverly Hills, CA: Sage, 1982. Blalock argues that much of social research is ill-conceived, because little attention is given to important conceptual issues.

———. *Basic Dilemmas in the Social Sciences.* Beverly Hills, CA: Sage, 1984. A wide range of problems that reduce the validity of social research is discussed.

Cicourel, Aaron V. *Method and Measurement in Sociology.* New York: The Free Press, 1964. Cicourel provides a classic statement on the need to develop measures that are culturally relevant, if accurate knowledge is to be procured through research.

Comas-Diaz, Lillian and Ezra E. H. Griffith (eds.). *Clinical Guidelines in Cross-Cultural Mental Health.* New York: John Wiley and Sons, 1988. The various "ethno-socio-cultural" factors that influence intervention with minorities are discussed.

Coulter, Jeff. *The Social Construction of the Mind.* Totowa, NJ: Rowman and Littlefield, 1979. An ethnomethodologically informed examination of reason is provided.

Denzin, Norman K. *The Research Act.* 3d ed. Englewood Cliffs, NJ: Prentice-Hall, 1989. Symbolic interactionism is adopted to facilitate a sophisticated theoretical discussion of the research process.

Douglas, Jack D. *Investigative Social Research: Individual and Team Field Research.* Beverly Hills, CA: Sage, 1976. An ethnographically sound portrayal of social research is offered.

Douglas, Jack D. *Creative Interviewing.* Beverly Hills, CA: Sage, 1985. Douglas explores the philosophical and conceptual issues associated with conducting socially relevant research.

Feleppa, Robert. *Convention, Translation, and Understanding.* Albany: State University of New York Press, 1988. A comprehensive study of the intricacies of cross-cultural understanding is undertaken.

Feyerabend, Paul. *Against Method.* London: Verso, 1978. The claim is made that the discovery of truth is elusive, and thus a multivalent approach to research should be encouraged.

Foucault, Michel. *The Birth of the Clinic.* New York: Vintage, 1975. An historical analysis is provided of how the "medicalization" of illness has occurred.

Foucault, Michel, *Madness and Civilization.* New York: Vintage Books, 1973. Foucault illustrates the adverse repercussions that occur when science comes to dominate discussions about disease.

Frankl, Viktor, *Doctor of the Soul.* New York: Alfred A. Knopf, 1963. The case is made that practitioners are not simply technicians and should try to avoid becoming reductionistic.

Giorgi, Amedo, *Psychology as a Human Science.* New York: Harper and Row, 1970. A theorist who is committed to phenomenology argues that psychology should not be viewed as a natural science.

Goffman, Erving. *Asylums.* Chicago: Aldine, 1961. Illustrated is the dehumanizing nature of mental hospitals.

Guattari, Felix. *Molecular Revolution.* Middlesex, England: Penguin, 1984. A key member of the anti-psychiatry movement exposes the way therapists operate as agents of "normalization."

Gudykunst, William B. and Young Yun Kim. *Communicating with Strangers.* Reading, MA: Addison-Wesley, 1984. A full range of concerns that are related to intercultural communication are mentioned.

Kinkaid, D. Lawrence (ed.). *Communication Theory: Eastern and Western Perspectives.* San Diego, CA: Academic Press, 1987. Discussed are the ways in which reality assumptions affect communication.

Kleinman, Arthur. *Patients and Healers in the Context of Culture.* Berkeley: University of California Press, 1980. The role culture plays in identifying and curing illness is given serious attention.

———. *Rethinking Psychiatry.* New York: The Free Press, 1988. Challenged is the standard idea that psychiatry should be viewed as an outgrowth of medicine.

Laing, R. D. *The Politics of Experience.* New York: Pantheon Books, 1967. A plea is made that the experiential dimension of mental illness should not be overlooked by practitioners.

Levine, E. S. and Amado Padilla. *Crossing Cultures in Therapy: Pluralistic Counseling for the Hispanic.* Monterey, CA: Brooks/Cole, 1980. Transcultural perspectives are described to improve the care received by Hispanic clients.

Lefley, Harriet P. and Paul Pedersen (eds.). *Cross-Cultural Training for Mental Health Professionals.* Springfield, IL: Charles C. Thomas, 1986. Based primarily on programs inaugurated in Miami, methods for training those who work in multiethnic settings are proposed.

Lincoln, Yvonna and Egon Guba. *Naturalistic Inquiry.* Beverly Hills, CA: Sage, 1985. A systematic analysis of qualitative research is provided.

Minkowski, Eugene. *Lived Time.* Evanston, IL: Northwestern University Press, 1970. Minkowski adopts an existential approach to understanding clients.

Miranda, Manuel R. and Harry H. L. Kitano (eds.) *Mental Health Research and Practice in Minority Communities: Development of Culturally Sensitive Training Programs.* Rockville, MD: National Institute of Mental Health, 1986. The aim of this volume is to encourage the development of "cultural competence" on the part of practitioners.

Murphy, John W. and Joseph J. Pilotta (eds.). *Qualitative Methods: Theory and Application*. Dubuque, IA: Kendall/Hunt, 1983. How qualitative research methods can be used in a variety of settings is the focus of attention.

Newton, Frank Cota-Robles, Esteban L. Olmedo, and Amado M. Padilla. *Hispanic Mental Health Research*. Berkeley: University of California Press, 1982. This volume supplies a bibliography of research related to the mental health of Hispanics.

Patton, Michael Quinn (ed.), *Culture and Evaluation*. San Francisco: Jossey-Bass, 1985. The cultural side of evaluation research is discussed from a variety of perspectives.

———. *How to Use Qualitative Methods in Evaluation*. Newbury Park, CA: Sage, 1987. The actual development of qualitative methods is explored in significant detail.

Pedersen, Paul. *Counseling Across Cultures*. Honolulu: University of Hawaii Press, 1981. Work conducted at the East-West Center on training culturally sensitive counselors is central to this book.

Pedersen, Paul B., Norman Sartorius, and Anthony J. Marsella. (eds.). *Mental Health Services: The Cross-Cultural Context*. Beverly Hills, CA: Sage, 1984. A wide range of issues is addressed pertaining to offering culturally-based services.

Pedersen, Paul (ed.). *Handbook of Cross-Cultural Counseling*.Westport, CT: Greenwood, 1985. Provided is a comprehensive picture of the issues associated with cross-cultural counseling.

Pollner, Melvin. *Mundane Reason*. New York: Cambridge University Press, 1987. Discussed is the social construction of reason.

Rabinow, Paul and William Sullivan (eds.). *Interpretive Social Science: A Reader*. Berkeley: University of California Press, 1979. The work of key authors who are advocates of interpretive social science is presented.

Radden, Jennifer. *Madness and Reason*. London: George Allen and Unwin, 1985. Radden discusses important philosophical issues related to the identification of madness.

Rogler, Lloyd H., Malgady, Robert G., and Rodriquez, Orlando. *Hispanics and Mental Health: A Framework For Research*. Malabar, FL: Krieger, 1989. A comprehensive discussion of the issues related to studying the mental health of Hispanics is provided.

Scheff, Thomas J. *Being Mentally Ill*. New York: Aldine, 1984. A host of social factors that mediate the identification of mental illness are discussed.

Scull, Andrew T. *Museums of Madness*. New York: St. Martin's Press, 1979. Provided is a history of how the mad have been controlled.

Scull, Andrew T. *Decarceration: Community Treatment and the Deviant*. New Brunswick, NJ: Rutgers University Press, 1984. Analyzed are the theoretical and practical implications of deinstitutionalization.

Sedgwick, Peter. *Psycho Politics*. New York: Harper and Row, 1982. The focus of attention are the political implications of traditional psychiatry and the anti-psychiatry movement.

Straus, Erwin W. *Phenomenological Psychology*. New York: Basic Books, 1966. Discussed are the basic theoretical tenets of phenomenological philosophy and their importance for psychology.

Sue, Derald Wing. *Counseling the Culturally Different*. New York: John Wiley and sons, 1981. The barriers that inhibit adequate intervention with minority groups are illustrated.

Sue, Stanley and Thom Moore (eds.). *The Pluralistic Society.* New York: Human Sciences Press, 1984. Developed is a minority perspective within the context of community psychology.

Szasz, Thomas S. *The Myth of Mental Illness.* New York: Harper and Row, 1961. A classic statement is made that refutes the physiological basis of mental illness.

Vega, William A. and Manuel R. Miranda (eds.). *Stress and Hispanic Mental Health.* Rockville, MD: DHHS Pub. No. (ADM) 85-1410, 1985. The relationship between stress, mental illness and the coping mechanisms used in the Hispanic community are addressed.

Wing, J. K. *Reasoning about Madness.* Oxford: Oxford University Press, 1978. Conceptual and other theoretical matters pertaining to identifying madness are given serious attention.

Wing, John K. and George Brown. *Institutionalism and Schizophrenia.* Cambridge: Cambridge University Press, 1970. Examined is the adverse impact of institutionalization on clients.

Index

Action research: description of, 130-133; versus elite model of research, 131
Antonovsky, Aaron, cognitive coherence, 74
Argyris, Chris, 132
"Ataque de nervios," 72

Barthes, Roland: innocent reading, 56; objectivity, 37; text, 47
Behaviorism: description of, 33-34; and the destruction of social reason, 34; and intervention, 34
Bernal, Martha E., 76
Binswanger, Ludwig, 36, 44, 45, 54, 56
Blumer, Herbert, 31
Bourdieu, Pierre, symbolic violence, 86-87
Buber, Martin, the interhuman realm, 45
Bureaucratic violence, 135

Canguilhem, Georges, 50
Catchment area: definition of, 4; and services to minorities, 9
Category fallacy, definition of, 72
Chavez, Nelba, 73; collision of mission, 79
Collins, Randall, 135
Comas-Diaz, Lillian, ethnocultural assessments, 69
Communicative competence, 86; definition of, 51, 120
Community, postmodern definition of, 54
Community-based agencies: and bureaucratic trap, 133; community relations, 134; and credentialism, 134; and linking-pin structure, 135-136; and organizational decentralization, 135; and the reduction of bureaucratic violence, 135; and scalar-chain of authority, 133
Community-based intervention: and appropriate funding mechanisms, 75-76; appropriate knowledge base for, 28-29, 46-48, 124; and community, 54, 125; and deprofessionalization, 125-127; and DSM-III, 24, 65; and dualism, 22-26, 44-46, 124; and facts, 48-49, 146; and the focus of intervention, 53-55, 92-95, 106, 147; and Grand theory, 26; and health, 53-54; and human action, 25, 27; and information playback, 120; and the medical model, 22; and methodology, 49-53, 130-133; and post-modernism, 38; and psychological realism, 33-37; and reflexivity, 55-57; and risk, 106; and social imagery, 27; and social networks, 78-79, 106-109; and sociological realism, 29-33; and theory, 37-39, 109; and therapy, 57; and training, 15, 78-79, 136-138

Community-based policies: and beliefs about social control, 149; and bureaucracy, 151-152; and the commodification of services, 144-145; and community involvement, 150-151; and the laissez-faire philosophy, 142-143; and the medical model, 147; and the privatization of health care, 75-76, 143-144; and the role of scientists, 146; and social pessimism, 148-149, 150; and social realism, 145-146; and the technological ethic, 147-148
Community Mental Health Movement: and appropriate needs assessment strategies, 10; changes in practitioners' roles, 7, 10-11; and the Civil Rights Movement 6; definition of, 2-3, 21; and definitions of community, 9-10; lack of minority professionals, 11-12; Mental Health Centers Act, 3; and minority services, 14-16; Omnibus Budget Reconciliation Act, 8; and President Carter, 12; and President Kennedy, 4-5; and prevention, 13-14; treatment philosophy of, 22-23
Comte, Auguste, 20, 49
Conflict theory: description of, 32-33; and mental illness, 33
Cross-cultural competence, definition of, 76-77
Cuellar, Jose, 74
Cultural broker, description of, 138
Cultural adaptation, of immigrants, 77-78
Cultural stereotypes, 74
Culturally sensitive training, 76-79

Davidson, Donald, passing theory, 54
Decision-making, traditional assumptions of, 96
Derrida, Jacques: and dualism, 31; and psychiatry, 24
Dole, Marie, 129
Double-loop learning, description of, 132-133
Double-rapport, definition of, 51
Dreyfus, Hubert, 91, 95, 96
Dreyfus, Stuart, 95, 96
Dualism: atomism, 93; bureaucracy, 94; critique of, 26, 44-46; data, 91, 92, 132; and decision-making, 45, 95-97; and epistemological pluralism, 100; the formalization of knowledge, 44-45; and human need, 90; and holism, 92; and ideology, 44-45, 56-57; macrodeterminism, 93; and medical model, 62; and mental illness, 88; and methodology, 132; and the mind, 96; norms, 98; objectivity, 44; realism, 49; reason, 88, 95-96; and rehabilitation, 98; standardization, 44-45; and technical competence, 45, 91; and treatment objectives, 52; and value-freedom, 46
Dunham, H. Warren, 6, 10
Durkheim, Emile, 30; and facts, 24; and pathology, 49

Edgerton, Robert B., 69
Ellul, Jacques, 55, 147
Epistemological Catchment Area Project, 65, 104
Epistemological participation, definition of, 54
Epistemological pluralism, definition of, 99-100
Etzioni, Amitai, 135
Eysenck, H. J., 22

Fanon, Frantz, 6
Faris, Robert E. L., 6
Felman, Shoshana, 88
Folk beliefs, and healers, 70-71
Foucault, Michel: and the biography of illness, 24; and critique of Cartesianism, 43; discursive formations, 49; and politics, 141-142; and reason, 88
Frankl, Victor, 36, 46, 54
Freudianism (briefer therapies): description of, 34; and intervention, 35; and perceived efficacy, 35
Friedson, Eliot, 127
Friere, Paulo, 6
Functionalism: critique of, 46; description of, 30-31; and mental illness, 31

Gadamer, Hans-Georg, fusion of horizons of interpretation, 51
Gebser, Jean: and centerlessness, 100; and systase, 94
Giorgi, Amedeo, 48
Goal Attainment Scaling, 52
Goffman, Erving, and frames, 49
Gouldner, Alvin, and reflexivity, 55
Greene, Barry R., 74

Heidegger, Martin, and *aletheia*, 48
Hispanic population, size of, 16
Horkheimer, Max, 45
Husserl, Edmund, 86

Ingleby, David, strong versus weak causality, 29
Intervention modalities, linkpersons, 115, 116; merienda, 115, 116, 118
Intervention models, description of, 106

Karno, Marvin, 69
Kesey, Ken, *One Flew over the Cuckoo's Nest*, 5
Key informant, versus key citizen, 90
Kleinman, Arthur, 2
Klerman, Gerald, 62, 63

Lacan, Jacques: illness and symbolism, 37; truth, 28
Lebensraum, 73
Lefley, Harriet P., 138
Levi-Strauss, Claude, social subconscious, 72
Levine, E. S., 70, 72
Lewin, Kurt, 17, 131
Likert, Rensis, 135
Luhmann, Niklas, and reflexivity, 55
Lyotard, Jean-Francois: terroristic intervention, 38; truth, 48

Malcolm X, 6
Marcuse, Herbert, affirmative culture, 53
Marx, Karl, 32
Maslow, Abraham, 36
Mead, G. H. 31
Mead, Margaret, 77
Medical model: and the Back to Basics Movement, 66; and clinical training, 66, 68; and ethnographic assessments, 69-72; and the philosophy of community mental health, 22, 64; and reductionism, 25, 63-64, 147; relevance for minorities, 65-66; and symptoms, 62
Medicalization: description of, 62-65; and medical training, 66-67; and the National Institute of Mental Health, 67
Mental Health Systems Act, 8
Mental illness: the category fallacy, 72; definitional difficulties, 21-22; ethnic beliefs about, 69; and ethnocultural assessments, 69-70; folk beliefs about, 70-71; and reason, 87-89; risk for, 73-74; and role strain, 30-31
Mid-town Manhattan study, 3
Miller, J. Hillis, truth, 37
Mills, C. Wright, 26, 147
Minkowski, Eugene, 49
Mirowsky, John, 62
Mosher, Loren, Soteria Project, 36
Multi-dimensional treatment planning, 127-130
Munoz, Ricardo F., 118

National Mental Health Act, 2
Nyswander, Vincent, 129

Omnibus Budget Reconciliation Act, 8

Padilla, Amado M., 70, 72, 76
Pareto, Vilfredo, reason versus nonreason, 88
Parsons, Talcott, 30, 49, 98
Polak, Paul, 36
Polanyi, Michael, tacit knowing, 130
Pollner, Melvin, mundane reason, 34
Postmodernism: basic tenets of, 37-39; communicative competence, 51; and community-based intervention, 38; and diagnostic judgments, 47, 49; facts, 49, 50; and language use, 47; local determinism, 49; and methodology, 50-53; and order, 53; and ratio-

nality, 88, 95-97; systase, 94; truth, 47, 48
Privatization: and community-based services, 143-144; and service delivery to minorities, 75
Program democratization, 133-136
Proyecto Bienestar: confianza, 107, 112; intervention design of, 114-116; linkperson network, 107, 115, 116; merienda intervention, 115-116; natural helpers, 106; policy implication of, 117-120; rationale for, 110-114; servidoras, 112, 114, 115; and social learning theory, 112
Public Law 94-63, 7-8

Reflexivity: description of, 55-57, 86, 123; and politics, 142; use of, 119
Risk proness, Mexican-American Women, 110-112
Roger, Carl, 36
Rogers, Edward S., 5
Rogers, Everette, 108
Roskin, Michael, 105
Ross, Catherine E., 62
Rothman, J. J., 77

Sabshin, Melvin, 10
Schutz, Alfred: life-plan of a community, 138; multiple realities, 54; null point, 88; reductionism, 89
Servidoras, 112, 114, 115, 116
Simon, Herbert, and rationality, 95
Social networks, 79-80, 106-109; confianza network, 107; linkperson structure, 107, 115, 116
Spencer, Herbert, 30
Stockman, David, 12
Straus, Erwin, 47
Sutherland, John W., 93
Symbolic interactionism: description of, 31-32; and mental illness, 31-33
Symbolic violence, definition of, 86-87
Systase: definition of, 94; implications for data collection, 95
Systems theory: and dehumanization, 94; description of, 93; and health, 97
Szapocznik, Jose, 78
Szasz, Thomas, 36

Third Force Psychology, 36
Technical competence: description of 24, 45; examples of, 89-90; limitations of, 91, 97, 120
Technological ethic, definition of, 147
Total institutions, political implications of, 5
Truth, traditional rendition of, 48

Valle, Ramon: cross-cultural competence, 76-77; linkperson network, 106; natural helpers, 114; social networks, 106

Wagenfeld, Morton O., 8
Weber, Max: critique of value-freedom, 91; interpretive adequacy, 56; rationalization of the world, 124
Weeks, John, 74
Weizenbaum, Joseph, 125
Winograd, Terry, 96

About the Authors

WILLIAM A. VEGA is Professor of Public Health at the University of California, Berkeley. He has published numerous articles on the subjects of minority mental health, psychosocial issues, and health promotion in diverse journals. In addition, he is the editor of *Stress and Hispanic Mental Health* and *Hispanic Natural Support Systems*.

JOHN W. MURPHY is Associate Professor of Sociology at the University of Miami, Coral Gables. He has contributed chapters, spoken, and published over 90 articles. In addition, he has published five books, including *Qualitative Methodology: Theory and Application—A Guide for the Social Practitioner.*